Elderstory 1
Who We Were

Compiled and Edited by

Gordon A. Long

AIRBORN PRESS
Delta, B. C.

Elderstory 1
Who We Were

Published by

AIRBORN PRESS

4958 10A Ave, Delta, B. C.

V4M 1X8

Canada

ISBN: 978-0-9952687-6-0

Printed by CreateSpace

Cover Design by Tania Mendoza

Cover photo courtesy of Garnet Barcelo, posted on his blog "Siam Longings" on Feb 13, 2014. All attempts have been made to determine the original owner of the image, to no avail. It is assumed to be the property of the estate of the professional photographer who was hired by the school to take the photo.

For the Families

This is a book of real stories about real people. ElderStory has requested that, wherever possible, storytellers get permission from people to use their names and stories. The stories remain the intellectual property of the storytellers. It is our hope and desire that no one will be hurt or offended by his or her portrayal in any of these tales.

For the Storytellers

These stories as published may not be exactly the same as the story you usually tell. It is the nature of folk tales that they change over time. You tell the story differently each time. People remember it differently. In the recording/transcribing/editing process, things get changed, especially if there is translation involved. But the story is still your story, and it is a story that people want to hear.

Thanks To

John Lusted and the KinVillage Association in Tsawwassen

Staff, students and families of Ecole Woodward Hill Elementary School, especially Lisa Anderson, Ravinder Grewal, Jas Kooner, Kelly Mcquillan and of course Elaine Vaughan, who organized our sessions.

Staff, students and families of Surrey Central Elementary School, especially principal James Pearce, and Sean Austin, John Kovach, Kevin Larking and Grace Jackson.

Staff and residents at the Langley Lodge Care Home

Pamela Chestnut, Mona, Tania Mendoza and Mercedes at DIVERSEcity.

Introduction

The ElderStory Project came about in a very natural way. So many people deeply regret not making a record of their family's stories before it was too late. And so those stories died with the people who told them.

Those of us on the Surrey Seniors Planning Table looked for a way to keep family stories moving down through the generations. It is good for children to know where they came from, who their families are. It leads to a sense of belonging and a stronger sense of self worth.

So we sought ways to enhance the telling of stories to keep family members and communities in contact with each other. And the ElderStory Project was born, with the intention of bringing the generations together through storytelling.

Our storytellers come from all walks of life, from all ages, from many cultural groups. Their histories originate in communities in rural Canada: in small villages in India and Iraq: in large towns and big cities around the world. But wherever they originate, the message always comes out the same. "Now we are here, and much though we love the places we came from, in this place we are happy."

The Surrey Seniors' Planning Table and DIVERSEcity Community Resources Society hope that you will enjoy these very Canadian stories.

Coming Soon

Elderstory 2: Who We Are – Coming in April
Elderstory 3: More Tales – Planned for Fall, 2017

Contents

1. Schools

1. Darryl Catton – The Trouble With School

I was born in Huntsville Ontario, and I was there until I joined the Air Force when I was 17. I went to school there. My wife and I went to the same school. We're both from the same area.

I went to a country school, you know, one of those schools with four or five grades in one room. I did all right in the country school, but then I moved to a town school because we moved to my grandfather's house and that was in town, so I had to go to the town school. That was a bigger school. My wife went there, too.

In school, I was always an instigator, a dreamer, get involved in anything, not pay attention, so I failed. Nowadays you don't fail. They give you lesser subjects, but those days you passed all the subjects or you stayed in that grade, and consequently I stayed in that grade. I failed twice. And I thought, because my father looked after the schools and he was a friend of the principal, I thought I could get a little special treatment but I didn't. I was sent for the strap a couple of times.

The principal's office, you went up through a door and up the steps, and I still remember that in my mind, because it was like going up to the gallows. His office was on the landing at the top. When you got sent up there, they used to strap in those days. I'd get sent up there, and he'd sit me down and pull the strap out and put it on the desk. I could always talk my way out of getting the strap. Because he was a friend of my father's and that. Almost always.

So I didn't do good in school, but I was asked to go over and play for the assembly for the high school when I was only in

1

Grade 8. And that was a kind of a privilege for my age. So I was kinda proud of that.

I threw the teacher's books behind his desk. They'd dare me to do things, and I was just trying to get in with the gang, you know, so I took all the books off his desk when he was out and threw them in the bin. I took the door off the principal's office and took it up and hid it in the attic. I hooked up a bell system. The old bells you know, I drilled holes in the floor. My father took me in to empty the wastebaskets, so I could get in. I knew which room I was in. In those days they rang the bells still to tell people that recess was over, or to move to the next room. There was just old bells. So I drilled a hole through there and ran some wires down. In the basement there was two wires running along the ceiling, low voltage wires, and I bared them and put a little loop on, and ran it up to this desk and tied it around the desk. Then just before I knew the bell was going to go I pulled it, and the bells would go and they would all disburse. Everybody would all get out early.

The principal, Miss Stewart – I knew her for years – she had an idea that it was me. She went to my father and said, "I think your son's ringing the bells." He went around and he took a flashlight, and he saw the whole thing. He went up, and it was right under my desk.

So he went and put two or three more batteries on this line and bypassed the bells. He said to Miss Stewart, "You just watch. When he hits his little wire he'll jump out of his desk." So she was waiting, and just before noon hour "Zip," I jumped up and they caught me right there.

And another time I told my teacher that I lost my mother's cheque, mother's allowance, you know. I said I lost it out in the playground, and that's all we live on, we've got three or four kids. So we went out and looked for it. Miss Spencer, she was pretty gullible. "We'll take the kids, and we'll find it." So we were out there for an hour.

I told the guys later. I said, "I never lost that cheque."

I was one of four kids, and you know when the kids go home from school, and they go, "What did you do in school?" and they start with the eldest, and I got fried, and I would stutter, because I had a lot to tell them, but it wasn't all good. And they'd get around to me and I couldn't get it out, or they wouldn't be interested, because they heard all the good stuff, so I got stuttering. People would come over and visit, and they'd always ask, "What grade are you in, son?" and I was 16 in Grade 8 or something. Stupid was a word that just riled me up for years. Everybody called me stupid.

So I think about it now, and jeez, those are some of the things I did. Nowadays, the things I did would probably get a kid expelled.

So anyway, I got out of school but I never graduated until I took night school. I wanted to get in the Air Force, but I didn't have the proper qualifications, so they told me to go home and take a course and get my Math up, which I did. Then I went back the next year and I got in the service. I was determined when I got into the service that I was going to buckle down and show them. Which I did. I took every course in the service I could; that's how I got the higher tickets. I'd go home and these same cronies I knew were sitting on the side of the street. And I was in uniform, and I was pretty proud of the fact that I made something of myself.

2.   White Flower – Primary Teaching

I started Elementary school in Niniveh. When I got to Grade 5, we moved to Baghdad. I continued Elementary in Baghdad. After Elementary I went to Art School. After that I became a teacher.

You ask about how many students in a class. I have taught 65 students in one class. Grade One Elementary. You know, when I came to Canada I took my grandchildren to the Elementary. "Oh, my goodness, just 25 children in one class!" But I taught 65. When I checked the duty, I said, "Oh, my goodness." Sometimes I didn't take a break; I stayed in the class to check the student's work.

I taught Religion in Grade 4, 5, and 6. Some people didn't like that I taught about Jesus. People, especially the Muslims, didn't like that.

In Grade 5 they started English. In private schools they start English in Grade 3.

I taught my class Arabic and Math in Grade 1. Another teacher taught Science and Social Studies.

It was too difficult for me when the children came and they didn't understand anything. I taught them the letters, I taught how to read, how to write. Very difficult, teaching Grade 1.

3. Joanne Harris – In the Classroom

The school I went to was a one-room school with grades 1 to 10 in it. We walked to school, two miles, there and back. It was fine in the summer time but in the winter it was wicked. My mother had to wrap me up to keep me warm. My brother, who was only a year and a half older, the same thing. If we'd get cold on our way home from school we'd stop in at a neighbour's to get warm, then proceed. Some children that lived on farms came to school on horseback. That was very useful for them, especially in the wintertime. Some had what they called a caboose drawn by horses, with a little heater inside if they had a great distance to come. It was just like a camper on sleighs in the wintertime.

There was a barn there, and some of these students were quite adept at looking after animals, you know, if they lived on a farm. They looked after their horses.

Grade 1 – 8 was taught by the teacher, but 9 and 10 you had to take through correspondence. It was hard. There were a lot of changes, not like here. We had different teachers, and some were better than others.

I particularly remember Grade 7. We had a man teacher, who was...I don't think he had proper training as a teacher. Mister Mitchell, his name was. He sat in a chair with his feet on the desk and he rarely talked to us. And one day I guess his

4

conscience bothered him, and he got up and he hit the blackboard with a piece of chalk, and he said, "Grades 1 to 10, I'm going to tell you the story of Rip van Winkle."

And you know, I've never forgotten that.

He was just there for a year, thank goodness, because he really wasn't a good teacher. The lady that followed him never stopped talking all day. She took up work with every grade and I really admired her and I realized what a difference it was from having had Mister Mitchell. This is the mystery. How did he get the job?

I remember a Miss Jones, and she did more talking. As a kid, I used to admire the jewelry that she wore. And she married a local farmer, something I wasn't going to do.

What I remember is there was a very large family living near the school, and they had a child coming to school every year. And there was always a Pencalla in school, from 1 to 10. I think they had about 13 children.

The school was just one room with all the desks lined up, and I think the most number of students that there were in that room was 30. The front of the room was all blackboards and chalk, and students were asked to volunteer to clear the blackboards after school, and clear the brushes. I think what they did was just bang the brushes together to get the chalk dust out of them. I don't remember doing that.

When you walked in the girl's cloakroom was on the right and the boys' cloakroom was on the left, and you left your little lunch pails in there. Usually they were three-pound lard pails. You had your initials punched out in the lid, at least my brother and I did, so you could never confuse your lunch pail with anybody else's. In the wintertime we often had a hot soup and I can't remember who would have made it, because that didn't concern me.

We started at nine o'clock in the morning we'd have recess for 15 minutes. An hour for lunch, and you'd be out playing pom pom pullaway, kick the can, baseball...you know.

That's about the only thing I was good at, playing softball. We didn't play volleyball or basketball or any of those things, because there was no gym, and you just didn't do it.

The teacher taught Reading, Writing, Arithmetic, Geography and History. Music Theory. I know the names of the lines and spaces. I know what a sharp is and a flat. Some taught Music. I took great patience in drawing the treble clef and the bass clef.

I remember having to draw a bowl of fruit, and I drew a big bowl, and the fruit was miniature. It was completely out of proportion. How did I know how to deal with that? We played musical chairs and other indoor games in the wintertime.

And we'd always have a Christmas concert. The parents would come to these concerts. I liked those concerts. We had to practise for them. We didn't have to do any schoolwork; we could do drama.

4. Cal Whitehead – Schooling at Home

I was the first boy. My older sister was a teacher to me. So I went to two schools. When she went to grade 1 and came home, that was time for me to go to "school." She taught me everything that went on in that school. So I could read at the Grade 5 level before I was even in Grade 1. That changed my life.

5. Marg Kennet – School in the Okanagan

Kids were not allowed to go to school until they were 7, because in Grade 1, I was at a one-room school three miles away, and we had to walk to and from.

It was a one-room school, grades one to eight, with a potbellied stove in the corner. The teacher was the same teacher that my Mum had for Grade 1, Mrs. Reedman. She kept in touch all through the years until just before she passed. She was friends with the family. I remember quite a few things about school life. We played anti–i-over, where you had a ball and you threw it over the peaked roof, to see if somebody could catch it on the other end. And games of tag and skipping and that.

And of course there were outhouses. Come Hallowe'en the boys, yes it was going to happen every year that they were going to dump over the outhouses.

It was really scary walking to school. Mainly I was frightened, even if I was with a couple of little kids. We were all little, under nine. And there were bear and there were coyotes, and it was pretty tough.

6. Ghidaa – Afraid to go to School in Iraq

I went to Elementary School. I finished Grade 5, and then we moved from one town to the other, and I could not continue my schooling. And then there were wars. Fear was the main problem. When they built a school later, I didn't go because I was afraid.

7. Hilda – Teaching in El Salvador

At school we had a different areas. There was a garden, there was a gym and when we went outside and played outside. Every year the teacher organized two events. The first was an exposition of manual arts. The second event was a dramatization and singing songs to the public. I was at elementary school for 6 years. I remember the name of my Primary Schoolteacher in the town of Apastepeque was Blanquita. She came from Spain. The teacher in San Salvador was a very special teacher. She taught us how to be responsible students.

Later I studied at a Secondary School in the capital of San Salvador, and then in Normal School for 4 years. This gave me all my high school qualifications and taught me to become a teacher.

I became a teacher of primary school first, and after I went to Don Bosco University to become a teacher of Science and Mathematics in Secondary School.

I finished working after 31 years of teaching. In elementary school one teacher covered all the subjects. Classes were about 30 students. In Secondary School, 40. Sometimes I taught night school. In El Salvadore people who don't finish the curriculum in childhood go to night school to learn.

After this experience I worked in a private school where they treasure the different values of the people. I worked 20 years in this school. I have good memories of the values this school gave me, and the values from my parents. I feel this second opportunity I had as a teacher was a special training for me in my life.

8. Charles – Junior High School in Taiwan

In the junior high school, to get from the farming village the transportation was not very convenient, so we had to walk from my home to the school. At that time the families had no money because we were poor, as were our relatives. We just walked without shoes because we had no money to buy shoes. So we walked a long distance in bare feet on crushed gravel streets. The road was not very good. We just walked there, three or four miles, and I think this was a good experience for me now. Because of all this walking, my feet were very strong. At that time, we did not worry; if we didn't wear shoes, we could still walk.

One time we went to school and there was a big storm, with big strong winds and I was worried. The dirt was flung into my eyes, and a tree suddenly fell down. I quickly moved to the side. Maybe this work helped me to protect myself from the winds and the stones and the leaves blowing against me. I didn't worry about those dangers because I knew how to protect myself.

So I think this is good for me to remember, now. When I meet some problem, I know how to protect myself because I have this experience.

9. NB – School in Al Qosh

I went to the village school in Al Qosh for Elementary school. It was a big building with many classes. It was a very good school. Iraq in the 60s and 70s it was a very good country.

There was peace; there was security. It was safe, but there were a lot of poor people. But everybody got to go to school.

But we left our village to go to Baghdad because my family was a large family with five boys and five girls, so we were a poor family. So we left our village to go to Baghdad because the level of life there, the chance to get work was better than our village. So we went to Baghdad and lived there.

In 1977 when I was 17 years old, I got married, and my husband was 27. I continued to learn in my High School. I finished it but I had to go through these years at High School. I had two sons, but they passed away because of the war with Iran and Iraq. My husband was not with me because he was in the front lines of the war. The war took eight years. All of these eight years my husband was in the war.

It was very, very difficult years in my life, because I lost my two sons and my husband wasn't there. I was alone with my three sisters. His parents were very attached to him, and to me also, but I feel like I was alone in this world. No one felt what I felt.

It was very, very difficult for me to lose my sons when my husband was away in the front lines, and the war, and I was in high school to study. Studying in Iraq is not like here. It is very difficult. It is very, very difficult, especially in Grade 12. Grade 12 is like you want to kill yourself. Very difficult. Work, work, work, and study and very difficult to pass Grade 12. I like a challenge in my life, and I passed the tests for Grade 12, and I got good enough marks to apply to university, but because of my difficult life I couldn't continue.

The high school in Iraq where I studied was a special school just for women who were married. The study there was very simple. Not focused on books and the curriculum. Not preparing for university, but just to get the basics. When you finish after Grade 12 you can apply to the university. They have the right to continue their education, no problem, but the study is not complicated, it is very simple.

My parents were Egyptian, but my father started a business in Ethiopia. I went to school there, a French-Canadian Catholic school. I was there until I finished grade 10. In the last two years I went to the English school, also in Addis Ababa.

When I finished high school I went to England. I studied at a boarding school for two years because I took Ordinary Levels in Ethiopia, and that did not get me to university. I needed another two years in England to get Advanced Levels. I got about 9 subjects in my O Levels, and then when I went to England I had to choose 3 subjects, depending on whether I wanted to go into Sciences or Arts. I chose Physics, Chemistry, and Zoology for my A Levels.

I went to a boarding school in Heddington, which is just outside Oxford. It was a girl's boarding school.

It wasn't fun. I thought I was a big girl, but I had to start from scratch. Too many rules and regulations. We were allowed three types of outings per semester. One with family and friends, one with my classmates, and I forget what the third one was. I had a friend there called Francois Levy, whom I just met last year in Paris, after about 50 years, which was interesting. I haven't kept in touch with the rest of my classmates.

When I was in boarding school we had different houses. We had to wear these horrible uniforms. We all looked the same, with bowler hats and ties. I belonged to Latimer house. Our colours were red and blue.

The whole Harry Potter experience.

I hated it. My parents were in Ethiopia and I was extremely lonely. I remember my first letters were 17 pages. Pages and pages of my experience. After that it was like two or three pages because I ran out of stuff to tell them, because there was nothing to tell them. Every Sunday we had to go for a walk in the cold, and I hate the cold as well. And then we had to write letters to our families. So, again, my letters were forced at that point, with nothing to say. We had to polish our shoes every

Sunday afternoon to get ready for school the next day. Just those standard routines.

My background was a problem at the beginning. It was in the 60s, and the short dresses were just coming in, so I shortened all my skirts to fit in. I was coloured, and my father made sure that I wasn't put in a room with another coloured girl. He didn't want us to be ostracized or separated. But they did put me in a room with a Nigerian girl. You know, we got along fine. It's not like I resented it. I felt like I wasn't white. I was called "café au lait." I did speak as well as they did, because I went to an English-speaking school. It was a French Canadian school, but everyone spoke English. But I hated it.

11. Carla Niemi – Changing Schools

My name is Carla Niemi. I'm the facilities manager here at DIVERSEcity Community resources society. I'm 57 years old. I am a second generation Canadian: Finnish, 100%. My grandparents moved to Thunder Bay, Ontario in the early 1900s. My parents were born there and they had six children.

My father unfortunately was kicked out of the house at the age of 13 after his 40-year-old father was killed by a train accident in Sudbury Ontario. At the age of 13 he went to the work camps, and there he became an alcoholic like many Finlanders in the area.

In Thunder Bay it's an area much like Finland, with a lot of logging, so there's work camps and the ladies cook and the men log, so that's where my parents met.

So my mother married an alcoholic, and she had a very hard life. During their marriage they had six children. I'm number 5 out of the 6. I started my schooling in Thunder Bay, Ontario. I did half of Grade 1 there. Then we moved to Kamloops, B. C. because my father had to leave the province in order not to go to jail, so he came to Vancouver and ended up in Kamloops, where he wrote to my mother love letters, which I've read and since destroyed.

So we joined him: a single mum and six kids and a box of sandwiches on the train and we came across Canada. So my second half of Grade 1 was in a school in Kamloops called Stuart Wood.

Because of my Dad's problem with the bottle, there were times when he lived with us and times when he didn't. Kudos to my Mum. She was the steady breadwinner and she would not allow him to live with us when he was drinking, so he only lived with us when he was sober. Where else he lived, I don't know. I'm a little girl, I don't know to ask.

Every time we lived in a different house – because we always rented – I'm in a new school. So I look at children today and "Oh, they've got to change schools!" It makes you a different kind of a person. It's not the end of the world.

I often changed schools in the middle of the school year, so I was in a different school. By Grade 4, I was changing schools. I begged my Mum, "Please let me finish the year." So I would walk past the school I'm supposed to attend, to get to the school I had been going to, in order to not change schools in April.

So then I changed schools for Grade 5 and half of Grade 6: we moved again too far away. Now I'm in a different school for Grade 6 and grade 7.

Then I went to Junior High. After one year we moved again, and I'm in another Junior High. And then I went to Kamloops Senior Secondary and in my Grade 10 year my Mum passed away.

So I'm the second youngest sibling. Looking back, when we look at the four months she was in hospital, I said to my little sister, who was 12, "Who made your lunches? Who bought our groceries? Who did your laundry?"

The time of our life was so traumatic none of us have memory of what happened. My older siblings already had marriages and children and didn't live in town, so I don't know how we survived that. But as an adult, I can tell you, I like change. I like moving. Nothing scares me, and if I am aware that I have a fear, I run to it to prove that there's nothing to fear. So that's how I live my life.

I started school at about 3 because I learned to talk very early. I was the second child. My eldest sister had the hard part of learning stuff. I just caught it and memorize everything because it's really easy for me to go through and in fact I've always done better than her at school.

I went to a private school, which had one room for kids of all ages, Of course being raised Roman Catholic our school was run by the nuns and anyone who's ever had to deal with the nuns knows they are very, very strict. You had to have absolute discipline. It serves me well because I still am very disciplined even now.

We did all the subjects. You had to memorize the tables, so you have to know 1x2 is 2. We knew the tune. I remember the tune very well, if I don't remember the words. It was fun. And you did the alphabet.

It was St. Joseph Girls' Primary, and then I went to the St. Joseph Convent, which was run by the Sisters of Cluny, which happened to be a French Order. They actually celebrated their 105th Anniversary of being in Trinidad in 1985. So, they had been there for quite a long time.

They had hired a teacher from Canada, from Quebec, a Ms. Pet. She did very well with us until she got married to a divorcée. That was the termination of her teaching contract. It was a scandal. A very bad example for us. So even though she was a good French teacher, her services were terminated because of that.

Basically, it was a British education because we used the same books that the children in England did. Like readers and so forth, you know, "Dan is the man in the van." Most of my friends who were in Britain read the same books. Even right through Primary School and secondary school, they were the same books. I had to write the Cambridge School Certificate Examination, the O levels and A levels. The Oxford and Cambridge exams, which I did. It was a very British education. Most of us, when we finish High School in Trinidad and graduated, went to either Cambridge or Oxford. Those were your choices. But I broke tradition and went to New York and I went to Columbia instead.

13. Mohammed Rafiq – School.

I was about five years old or so when I started going to school. My Dad being busy in his job, he sent somebody to take me to the schoolmaster, and he entered me in the register as a student in the school. I have some vague memories of that time, but quite clearly about some incidents and also the environment that we had in the school particularly.

We had to take our own mats to sit on. Our school had a few rooms, and the rest of it was sitting under the trees and getting our education. I believe it was one particular neem tree under which our class was held. Under that we had our classes on the mats. Our teachers were very simple but very dedicated teachers. They gave us the best education I can remember, in all aspects. It's not only the factual information that they gave. They were also character builders as teachers, as substitute parents they taught us how to behave at that time too, in our early years. From there our Primary school was from Grade 1 to Grade 5 and from there on went into the High School.

There our classes basically we had a room, but most of the classes during the summer months were held under the trees because it was better environment there for sitting. Our teachers took us through various grades. Again, I must say that we were so lucky that the teachers were teaching us all aspects, all points of view, and they gave us the best education that we could have at that time.

I went up to Grade 10 in that school, and I had two elder brothers who were going through the same school, and they were very good in their studies. They were on the Honour Roll of the school. Then here I came, and I was the naughtiest boy in the class. My teachers would get upset. "How come your brothers are so studious and they're on the Honour Roll, and you are dragging along, barely passing every class?"

14

Anyway, I came to my senses when I was in Grade 9, and I started studying and I got very good grades in Grade 10. From there on I forgot about the naughty stuff that I did and became a serious student at that stage.

I think the naughtiness that we did was that we teased our teachers. We did all sorts of stuff when they were not around. We had all kinds of characters in the class, and everybody would be doing their thing, like teaching Bollywood-type dance steps to others, and teasing, and all kinds of stuff we did. But that is probably normal in the young age for anybody.

But I'm glad that we went through that in a very nice way. I was very lucky that all my classfellows, I don't know the reasons to this day, but they were very good friends of mine, very friendly and protective from all kind of hooliganism that others were doing at that time. I am still thankful to them. Maybe I was innocent or whatever it was, something attracted my classfellows and they were very protective to me.

After Grade 10 we went into the College and did my FSc – Fellowship of Science. It is just a degree before BSc, in the same sequence like FSc, BSc and MSc. So we had FSc, which was the equivalent to Grade 12 in Science.

So I had the subjects of Chemistry, Physics and Biology in that and then from there on I went to Lahore and did my BSc and my MSc from Punjab University in Botany.

14. Mohammed Rafiq – School Misdemeanours.

Some naughty stuff that we did in the school was, one time we had a very simple Math teacher. When he came in the class, he would take his shoes and his hat off and put them aside. One day we decided to steal both those things, and went out when the class was finished, and locked the door from outside with the bolt. And the guy was just sort of jumping around trying to find his things and knocking at the door so he could come out. Finally someone opened the door, and he came and he scolded the heck out of us.

At one time my brother, I don't know where he found out, learned that there were two chemicals, I don't remember their

15

names, but when you put them together, they would change to the colour red. What we did was we threw the colour on somebody's clothes, and they would be all messed up, but in a minute or two all that would evaporate. I did that; I got it from by brother and I threw it on somebody's white shirt. It was all red, and he was so mad, he went scolding to the teacher.

By the time he reached the teacher the colour was gone, and he was looking, "Where is that red colour?" So the teacher found out and beat the heck out of me for doing that. Those are the type of things we were doing.

We had some small windows at the top of the room to get the hot air out, and we were just jumping around and somebody was looking into the window, and I pushed his head into it, and he broke the window and scattered the glass all over the class that was happening inside.

We had tennis balls and we would throw them through the open windows and run away. There were so many naughty things that we did. Nothing too serious.

Right beside our school there was a girl's school. The wall between the high school and the girls' school was made of mud. Somebody had made a hole at the base of the wall. Both boys and girls used to tease each other through those holes.

One time I was sitting with a friend of mine by that wall during the winter months, because that was where the sunshine and the warmth would be, and some girl poked her hand through the hole. So we grabbed her hand. She had bangles on her hand, and we took them all off. She was trying to pull the hand, and it wouldn't go anywhere.

In the meantime a teacher came. He wanted to know what we were doing there. We held her hand behind our backs. She couldn't cry or say anything because she would get in trouble too. We never found out who it was. We couldn't give back the bangles because we didn't know who she was. The girl went away, and there we were with the bangles in our hands.

So in spite of all that had happened to the family we still had some youth left.

15. Brenda Casey – I. L. Peretz School

I went to an elementary school that was uniquely a Jewish elementary school. It was considered a humanistic, Zionist, humanitarian school, so it was very socialist. The name of the School was I. L. Peretz. He was a quite a famous writer in Jewish traditions. He wrote in Yiddish. He was an extreme Zionist who also believed that the religion had a certain amount to offer in terms of faith but that the real core of Judaism had to do with the cultural backgrounds of the people, and that was going to keep them connected and keep them flourishing.

So the school was based on a very egalitarian system and also one in which people were to understand and appreciate differences, although everybody at the school was Jewish, except for one teacher whose children also went to the school. She was not Jewish, but she just decided that she wanted her kids to have a Jewish education.

All our teachers were qualified teachers but many of them were Holocaust survivors, so we learned, I think, too young about the Holocaust.

I started in what was called Low Kindergarten, so it would be called Nursery school now. I started when I was three years old and so by the time I was four I spoke Yiddish quite fluently because we spoke Yiddish half a day and English half a day. In Grade 4 they introduced Hebrew, so there was a quarter of a day Hebrew, a quarter of a day Yiddish and half a day English. And in Grade 7 we had a quarter of a day in French, quarter of a day, English, a quarter of a day Yiddish and a quarter of a day Hebrew. So by the time we finished Grade 7 we had four languages, three of them very well set. The French was basic, and I continued with that in High School.

Then we went to a public High School, but the experience in a traditionally Jewish environment was that I learned about history. When we learned Bible Studies you didn't learn Bible Studies as a religious experience, we learned it as the history of the Jewish people. So in my mind Moses was around, but I

17

never got to meet him. It was that kind of thinking. It was very naïve in some ways, but it was somewhat helpful, in that Bible stories were more like my history, rather than something that was based in faith.

When I went to public school, it was the first time I got to know a lot of kids who were not Jewish. I had one very good friend who was not Jewish. She went to a Lutheran church. She lived right nearby. But she came to the YMHA, the Young Men's Hebrew Association where our activities were. She went to Jewish camps in the summer. She dated Jewish boys when she got older.

In our youth we just thought she was a different kind of Jewish, it was just so all-inclusive.

So going to high school was when I first really met kids from other countries and other cultures. It was a new experience to learn that not everybody was Jewish. It was a whole new way of life.

16. Graham Mallett – Dad's Breakdown

I was born in New South Wales, Australia. When I was five, we moved to a little settlement called The Risk. There was a two-room school there. My father taught at that. During the war they were very short of teachers, so he had 60 kids in a couple of rooms for a couple of years, so he had a breakdown, and then they gave him another teacher and he kinda survived it.

Mental health wasn't recognized as it is today. He described it as a nervous breakdown. I remember him talking about it later. I don't remember too much of the symptoms at the time. He was pretty edgy; I remember that.

As part of this, I think, he got Bell's Palsy, when the nerves on one side of your face stop working. His face all collapsed, because the muscles wouldn't work, and they were trying to fix it. I remember it was a dentist who was a good friend of my father who came up to the hospital. What they used to do in those days they would hook something in the corner of the patient's mouth and hook it back over his ear while the face healed. But then there was a young medical student in the hospital, and he said, "I just read about something where they had a dental plate that had a little hook on it." So my father asked his dentist friend, and he said, "I'll have a shot and try and make you one." And so he did, and it worked. It looked like a tusk.

He went back to work immediately. They were so short of teachers and they couldn't get anyone else.

17. Fayza Massour – School in Iraq

I studied in Syria from Grade One to Grade 12, the Baccalaureate. The high school was all girls, without boys. It was a government school, all girls. Twenty-five to thirty students per class. Silent. Syria was very advanced in that way. The teacher kept us in silence, and the girls were also very good.

18. Yuliya Badayeva – School in Ukraine

I had a good time. I was going to school with my cousin who was pretty much like my sister. We lived in the same courtyard, and we went to the same kindergarten, the same school, and that was really nice.

The school, kindergarten, I remember sleeping a lot during the day. The food was pretty decent. Playing was fun, too. I liked it, but I do feel that we were pretty privileged family while I was growing up. I got the opportunity to go to a really good kindergarten. There was a good community between the parents and the kids, and a lot of people knew each other.

We watched a few videos recently, because we converted a lot of our VCR tapes to CD. So for example, March 8 is International Women's Day, like Mum's day. One thing that I think is different from school here is that we often had presentations in front of the parents, and we would practice little songs, and we'd have outfits made for us, and it was really fun. So March 8 we had International Women's Day, and we had one for New Year's.

Our school was called a Lycée, from Grade 1 to 11, and maybe now they have grade 12 there. The buildings were made out of brick.

That's actually something we noticed when we came here. A lot of buildings are made out of wood, and we were like, "What? That's not sturdy at all." And I guess brick insulates differently.

It's a bit different there as well because you have one class and you all stick together, and you go to all of your different classes together. There was Grade 1A and 1B. You would be with 1A; there were about 30 kids in one class, and you'd have the same schedule with the same 30 kids.

As we went along, there were more subjects, and more different teachers. In Grade Three we started learning Russian, and English was from Grade One. All different teachers. PE was a different teacher, right from the beginning.

My Mum was surprised here. How could one Elementary teacher cover everything: PE and Math? It was totally different.

I remember some aspects of school were more fun for me, because I had known the people for a long time, so it was more fun.

There was always a lot of homework. I came to Canada in Grade 4 and I didn't study for Math at all until Grade 8 because we had already covered that material. I was like, "We already did this in Grade 2."

19. Olena Chemeris – School in Ukraine

I went to Kindergarten in the '70s. It was totally different from what Canadian Kindergarten looks like. It was a separate building, a completely self-contained facility, two stories. They had a kitchen, a laundry, and different classes. All the kids were separated into groups, divided by age, and these groups, when I started at 4, I would stay in this group and would go in this group until age of 7. So for three years I was with the same group. Maybe some kids in and out, but pretty much the same group.

We had two teachers. One for morning hours, another for afternoon hours, and we also had Nanny. We would call her Nanny. Because what's different from in Canada, we didn't bring food to Kindergarten. It was cooked there. So Nanny would take care of us. She would serve the food and she would clean up.

So we would come to Kindergarten in the morning and we would have breakfast. After breakfast we would have classes, like alphabet, or we would sing these songs, or I remember we would learn the days of the week, the calendar.

Then we would go out and play outside. Then we would come back and have dinner. We had a separate room with beds, and after dinner we would go and sleep. After sleep we would come back for a snack. Before going home we would have supper. So it was totally, four meals the whole day. Child care up until 6 o'clock when parents came home from work.

At 7 years old you go to Elementary School, Grade 1 to 3. There were about 30 people in the class, with one teacher.

Also in Elementary school you would come at 8:30, and if you had nobody to watch you after the class finished at 2, you would stay in school with a different teacher. After school child care. If you had someone to take care of you, you went home after classes.

Grade 4 to 8 was middle school. More subjects, but you were still in your class of 30 people. You would go to different teachers for different subjects, with the same group of people. That's why I think it was good. You made your friends in the group.

After Grade 8 it was Secondary. You had the choice: continue into High School, or go into Trade School, at a separate school, where they would teach you a profession.

I liked the group I was in. There was always some event going on. We would get together and have competitions, some part of the cultural life. "Which class is the best singers of World War II songs?" or something like that.

20. Maria – Mathematics Teacher in Iraq

I finished elementary school in Mosul, and after that, Secondary and high school in Baghdad, and my university also in Baghdad. I became a teacher of Mathematics in High School, and taught for 27 years. The Mathematics book in high school is the same in all of Iraq. Nothing different from city to city. Before, there were between 35 to 40 or 42 students in a class in Elementary and High School. Now there may be 100 students in a class.

21. Nagham – School in Iraq

I was 6 years old when I went to Elementary School. I finished half way through High School, and then went into Commerce at the age of 16. It was a special stream in regular High School. Then I got a job in Import and Export business. An Accounting position because of my training.

22. Awatif Matti – School in Mosul

I learned in Mosul from Grade 1 until I finished university in 1976. After that I worked in a cement company, working on chequing and accounting. Then in 2005 I went to another company that made medicine. The same work.

I went to university to train for this. I studied Accounting and Administration at university. While I was working, I lived at home with my parents.

23. Eeman Yousef – School in Iran

I went to school when I was six years old at Grade 1, and when I was 12 I left. Then I started working in hairdressing at 20. An Egyptian lady trained me at her shop.

24. Susan Kuo – School in Taiwan

I was born in a small town on the northeast side of Taiwan, but in our town there are no good schools. So the best Junior high school in our county was away from our home. We needed to take the train for one hour from my town to the school. On the train they had so many people from different small towns. From the station, we had to walk 30 minutes to the school. At that time, we liked going to school, when there were no typhoon holidays.

Nowadays children are very happy if the weather is not good. They are happy to have no school that day. In our day, we always liked to walk, to go to school. We took the train. If the train could not go through the town because of flooding from a typhoon, then we would walk in the water.

There were several stops from our town to the school. When I was a teenager, we got on at the first stop, so we always had seats. But in the middle there were so many young guys who were standing up in front of us. It was like dating at times. We had a little social connection. It was a lot of fun.

It's a good memory. We did this for 6 years, from Junior High to Senior High.

25. Gordon Long – Decker Lake Elementary School.

We lived in a farming community called Palling, and in the late '50s we had to take the school bus to the next town to go to school. Decker Lake Elementary had two classrooms, with washrooms and a furnace room (coal furnace) in between. There was a tiny room off the Grade 4 – 6 classroom that served as a medical room and staff room. We had those old-fashioned desks that were screwed in rows to a couple of rails, and you sat on a bench hinged to the desk of the student behind you. We had inkwells and nib pens, which I recall making a lot of mess with. I was always fiddling with things.

We had from grades 1 to 6 with two teachers. I have no idea how many kids there were, but it must have got crowded, because when I hit Grade 6 they moved my class to Burns Lake Elementary, 6 miles farther away.

It was a pretty standard school. I saw a picture recently of a classroom in Minnesota from the same era, and except for having George Washington on the wall instead of Queen Elizabeth, it was identical, right down to the design of the light fixtures!

One thing I always remember, our Intermediate teacher, Mrs. McCormick, got migraines. If she had a headache, she would give us work to do and go and lie down in the medical room. Now, my class at that time was not a choir of angels. We had some pretty rowdy farm boys, and I wasn't calm, myself. But let me tell you, we sat as quiet as churchmice for the rest of the day. She was a great teacher, and we had a lot of respect for her. When the chips were down, everybody rallied round.

For playground equipment we had see-saws and tall swings and a softball backstop. We played a game called "scrub," which was like softball, except there were only three batters. When a batter was put out, he or she went into the outfield, the catcher moved up to batter, and all the base players moved around one position. It was sure a good game for training everyone to play every position and only needed about seven kids to play. If there were less, we only had two batters.

Unfortunately, there wasn't much else to do, and a lot of the "games" involved demonstrating physical dominance over the other guy. The standard form was wrestling, where the object was to pin the other person, usually by forcing him to his back and sitting on his chest, holding his arms down with one knee on either shoulder. In theory the loser said, "Give," and the winner let the loser up, but the bullies (and there were several) weren't so fussy about the rules. I still get claustrophobic if I ever get pinned on my back and can't move. Like at the dentist.

Just to give an idea of the kind of atmosphere that reigned on the playground. When I was in Grade 1, I was a pretty strong kid. I was brought up in a logging camp with only my older brother for a companion, and we worked and wrestled and kept ourselves pretty busy.

The first week of school a couple of the older boys got hold of me and told me that if I was going to get on in this school, I had to "take on" Julie Evans, the toughest girl in Grade Three.

Now, I wasn't completely stupid. Julie Evans was a nice, cute girl, considerably larger than me, but I liked her. She certainly wasn't mean, and she had never been anything but nice to me. But they assured me that she was the one I had to beat.

She was standing up on the porch, which was about 6 steps high, with her friends. I swaggered up there, and I don't remember what stupidity I said, but I indicated that the porch wasn't big enough for the two of us. She, not realizing who she was dealing with, answered in kind, and in the end I pushed her off the porch and down the steps. She didn't fall or get hurt or anything, because my heart wasn't in it, and I knew the moment we locked horns that I was stronger than she was.

Well, word got around. I mean, if one of those guys would have pushed me off the porch, nobody would have batted an eye, but I guess chivalry was the order of the day, and I had stepped over the line.

So the teacher took me into her classroom and reached down into the drawer of her desk and pulled out what looked suspiciously like a piece of belting from my Dad's sawmill. This was "The Strap," she told me, and it was used on people who started fights.

So if Julie, nee Evans, from Decker Lake ever reads this story, I want her to know that I have never, ever picked a fight with anyone else in my life.

2. Everyday Life Then and Now

1. Middy Lundy – First Job: Selling Doughnuts

Every kid wants more money. I don't know where I heard of it, but young people could sell doughnuts over the phone. So I applied for the job and sure enough I got it. Of course.

Well, I phoned and I phoned and of course you start with all your friends and family, but after a while they sort of, you know, don't like you as much.

That's where you start, but then you branch out because you're getting desperate because you're not doing any sales. And that doesn't work either.

So the final pitch to the whole thing was our family. We ate doughnuts for ages. I don't know what it cost my mother to buy all my merchandise. It was heavy.

I lasted probably one morning.

Oh, my, I'm 90 now, and I was, say, 10 then, so this happened 80 years ago. They were just little jobs like that when we were young. Christmas cards or something. You'd try anything you could do, you know, but in unfortunately I wasn't too successful with any of them.

2. Cal Whitehead – Kids on the Street

When the Depression started, the bank my parents had their money in went belly up. So here they were with four preschool children right at the beginning of the depression. The bank eventually paid out 10 cents on the dollar and that gave my parents enough to make a down payment on a house on the western edge of the city of Vancouver. We used to play on the street. It was a boulevard street, with parking room and strips of grass and trees about 15 feet wide on either side of the street. This street was made out of concrete. And every 15 feet there was a mark. So when we played out on the street, we played who owned which mark.

At certain time of the day when we were playing on the street, mothers would come out and call their children. My mother never called. She came and stayed on the porch looking at us. And when one of us caught her eye, she knew we would come in for dinner.

One of the women was the daughter of a dairy owner and married to the head of the dairy, she used a cowbell and it went "gong, gong, gong, gong," and the boy and girl knew they were to go in. Another one used a whistle, like a referee's whistle. The intensity of the blowing told those kids something. Those are the ones that I remember. Everyone broke up at that point. I owned a baseball and bat and I took them in to the house. Later I took my football into the house. Anyway, we were all kids growing up together, interacting.

3. Darryl Catton – Growing up in the Country.

When I was a kid in 1944, we lived in a little house. I was born in a place called West Road. The house sat back from the driveway and at the end of the house there was a big garage. The house is still there. We didn't have any running water or electric light, just coal oil lamps. We also didn't have any phone or a car. In this day and age that is hard to imagine. We eventually got all of these things. I remember the first phone. It sat on the wall, and it had a little crank on it. You had to turn the crank and it would ring the line, and you could hear. And when you were on the line you could hear clicks, with people listening on the line to what you were saying. So they got to know your conversation. It was good for gossip.

The first car my father had was a black Ford. We called it a puddle jumper. It had a seat in the back that was open to the air called a rumble seat, where we kids would ride.

We also had a hand pump installed in the kitchen on the counter so my mother wouldn't have to carry water from the well, which we normally did. We had an old wood stove, and the heat came from the basement. They had no duct pipes; the heat just flowed up through the floor through big grates. You'd have to go and restoke it every morning.

We also had a backhouse toilet, so at night we all had a big chamber pot that we had under the bed to pee in. We were supposed to get up and go outside the house for our other duties, but that wasn't always the case during the cold, so you can imagine the smell on those cold winter days.

4. Darryl Catton – On the railway tracks

When I was a kid we lived close to the railroad tracks, and just after the Depression, there were still people wandering around from the west and that. Good people, just had bad luck. And they'd come up to my mother's house, and they'd knock on the door. She wouldn't let them in, but she'd give them a little work and something to eat. And they'd do a few little things around the house and around the yard. We were kinda scared of them, because they were called hobos, you know. Years later I met a lot of people like that, who were on the tracks who became well-to-do people.

But this one particular person came back to my mother years later, drove up into the driveway in a big car, and he went to the back and pulled out a Daisy BB gun and brought it up and gave it to me. He had a big white moustache and one of those Panama hats. Big tall guy. He introduced himself to my mother. "I was one of the guys. I came back to your place several times, and you were always congenial with me." And he gave her stuff.

That's one of the stories I remember as a kid. It stuck because of that BB gun.

5. Marg Kennet– Grandma's Fall

I found this clipping after my Dad died. It was a column in the Salmon Arm Observer in 1912 or 14. "Mrs. F. Peachey of Canoe had the misfortune to fall backwards into the cellar through the door in the floor, which she had by accident left open. Her little boy Wilfred always makes it a point to close it after her, but this time he had forgotten to do so. As it was getting dark in the kitchen she didn't notice that the door was

28

not closed and she received a rather serious injury and is now confined to bed, unable to move.

I don't know what the injury was. Haven't a clue.

6. Jamie Long – Shooting

We grew up in the bush as you will probably pick up, and guns were one of those things, just part of life. We had a broom closet in the porch; the doors were never locked, and the guns were all in the broom closet. Shotguns, rifles of all sorts and descriptions.

I remember quite typically, I must have been maybe seven or eight years old, and my brothers were six or seven years older than me, and after church we'd come home, and Mum would make a big Sunday dinner, and Dad would bring out a box of .22 shorts, and we had a kind of a screen to screen our garbage dump out back of the house, which was typical of everybody, and we had a kind of a fence, there, and we'd pick up all the bottles that had accumulated over the week, and Dad would take us out there and he had sort of a method.

Here I'm a young kid, seven or eight years old, with a .22, and even with a short shell you could do a lot of damage, but the deal was that he had a toe scratch line, and when it was your turn you had the breech open – Dad always had us with the breech open – and then he'd give you the shell, and you'd step to the line, keeping the gun pointed towards the garbage dump, never waving it around, then you'd put your shell in and you'd take your shot. Then you'd open up your breech and return the gun to the porch, then you'd wait for your brothers to take their shots, and then we'd all go up and see how we did. Simple, standard Army training that Dad instilled in us, and he explained exactly how important it was that we didn't mess it up.

So by the time I was about nine or ten I wanted to go hunting grouse, and Dad said, "Go ahead, but stay away from the highway. Don't go anywhere near the highway. And no friends. No friends are to go with you. If you're hunting you can take Bimbo the dog, but you can't take any friends."

29

So I'd go out there and pop a few grouse and I'd shoot squirrels and whatever I could do. You know, I wasn't a very good shot at the time, I was okay, but I don't think I really had the killer instinct. It didn't really matter to me if I killed anything or not. But I did come home with grouse sometimes, but then I'd have to pluck 'em and I didn't really like the taste of grouse that much, so I didn't do it that often.

So when I was about ten or so, up from Wenatchee, Washington comes this American family who moves into the old farm down the road that once belonged to Jo Smith, my godmother. They had two boys, David and Mike. David was my age. Mike was a year older. And this was a marvellous thing. Two new friends showed up, whatever.

So this one day I was out there with my gun, as I often was. I went out with the .22 after school lots of times. And it just so happened that David had dropped by with his bike, and there I was with the .22. Dave said, "Where are you going?"

"Hunting."

He said, "Can I come?"

I said, "No, no, you can't come, because my Dad says that nobody can go with me when I'm hunting. I'm supposed to be by myself."

"Aw, come on," said Dave. "Come on."

Now he was a new kid, and he was from the States, which was bigger and larger than life for me, and I sort of wanted to impress him and whatever else. So I said, "Okay, but don't tell your Dad or Mum or don't tell anybody."

So we go out there, and me showin' off and bein' the showoff that I was, I go out there and I plug three grouse. David was absolutely blown away. He couldn't hit the broad side of a barn at the time. He was a hopeless shot. And I'd been at it for quite a few years. I was a decent shot.

David was really impressed, so I sent him home with two grouse, like a damned fool, so I gave up the gig. He went home with two grouse, and I came home with one, because I didn't want to pluck it and I didn't really like grouse, anyway.

But can you believe it, Bill Fountain in his greatness as a parent, I guess he liked the grouse quite a bit, he figures that if little Jamie Long can do that, then his boys could do that. So what does he do the next weekend? He goes out there and buys two brand-new Cooeys for David and Mike, and gets them a bunch of shells, and, "Away you go, boys." With no training whatsoever.

So a couple of days later David and Larry Klassen, who lived just below the Fountain place about a mile down the road from me, they go out hunting together. David is all poised because he can see a rabbit across the fence, and Larry at the moment is stepping through the fence, and he'd stepped through the barbed wire fence, and he stood up just when David shot. It hit him in the right temple and the bullet ran all the way around his skull underneath the skin and came out behind his left ear. And he was still ambulatory. In fact, he ran down to Highway 16 and hitchhiked the 9 miles into town to get looked after.

So guess what happened to me and my gun? My ability to go hunting was taken away, too. I wasn't allowed to go hunting after that, but I did end up going hunting with my Dad. Shot my first moose when I was 15, I think it was.

7. Marg Kennet – Art's Folly

My father-in-law's name was Art, and Art had a very interesting incident. It involved his vehicle that was parked in an underground parkade of a condo building in West Vancouver. I adored my father-in-law. He was a very bright, organized guy whom this type of incident was most unlikely to happen to, but it did.

One day Art decided he was going to go into the trunk of his car because there was a malfunction of the taillight, and he knew he could fix that.

He was a tall man, about six feet, and he gets his body into the trunk of this car, and he's way over in the corner and his bum hits the trunk lid, and it was an automatic closing trunk. So before Art knew it, he could not turn around and stop this process. His arms were above his head, and he was locked in the trunk.

A little background is that Art had a very serious heart condition. So being in this type of situation was really, really dangerous. He did have some nitro in his pocket. He was there for 15 minutes, and nobody came out of the elevator, so there he was. After about 15 minutes he heard the elevator, and he heard, "clip clop, clip clop," coming out of the elevator, so he knew it was a lady.

So he said, "Ma'am, it's Art Tenet. Would you mind going upstairs and having Maisie bring down the keys because I'm locked in the trunk."

This woman said, "Whoa. I'm going to get the manager." She was totally freaked out. This was not something she wanted to get involved in.

It took another five to ten minutes. My mother-in-law was just beside herself when she knew that Art was in the trunk and air was scarce and he might have a heart attack.

She's got Parkinson's, and it's just going ape. Poor Maisie is just beside herself.

So they opened the trunk and out comes Art. And he's really quite composed. And nobody can believe it. And they said, "Art, how do you feel?"

And he said, "Well, actually, I didn't even have to take a nitro."

8. Evelyn Wallenborn – My Connection with Seniors

Through my life I have always had a close association with seniors.

When I was a youngster my grandmother lived with us. She loved to make braided rugs out of rags. She would tell us stories of "the old country" meaning the Ukraine. She taught me a Ukrainian prayer that I still recite nightly. In the country in Manitoba I would have to walk to the Post Office about 1 mile (as the crow flies), mail came in twice a week and I would pass by a widow's house. I would always stop in to see how she was doing or if she needed groceries. Another widow in the area was afraid to be alone at night, so me and my sister took turns to stay with her and go to school from there. In Utah I met another widowed senior and we would spend time together and I would shop for her. It was always hard to leave from there as she would expect me to stay longer.

After we moved from the States, we lived in Burnaby for 4 years and also had senior neighbours which we had good connections with.

In Surrey, I re-connected with a senior I knew from Britannia days; there again it was tea and talk of old times.

I feel that my connection with seniors was a learning experience as they recite their early years. These are memories I will always treasure.

Now, I am a senior and am fortunate to have a neighbour's two children to spend time with me. They call me Grandma and we have great times together. An expression they use is "Not everyone is so fortunate to have their Grandma living next door."

I have volunteered for the Surrey Seniors' Planning Table for 9 years now, so I still have a senior connection.

9. Marg Kennet – Hallowe'en Hi-Jinks

I became a social worker in 1966 and started work in Kamloops, which was a great place for a young person to be. There were a lot of young people, working people there. I didn't have a place to stay because I only had about ten days notice that I was going to be posted there. So my supervisor arranged for accommodation for me, and it happened to be right next to Shoening's Funeral Parlour. Apparently this place had not had a very good reputation, but they'd cleaned it all out and it was fine when we got there.

I had two roommates that I didn't know who turned out to be delightful. They were both from Victoria, as was I. They were teachers. We just had a great time, the three of us. We were always playing practical jokes on one another and had a great social life, and everything was wonderful.

Above us in the apartment were two young guys. One was an RCMP officer, and the other guy worked at the funeral parlour. The funeral parlour owner didn't like us very much because we used to have the odd party and there was the whole funeral parlour parking lot that our guests could park in. I don't think that anything very active was going to be happening in the hours that we were partying, but nine times out of ten he would knock on our door, and everybody would have to find other parking. He just had to do it. He wasn't necessarily our best friend.

In the parking lot of the funeral parlour was this great big clock that was mounted on a post. It was huge. It had a light on it. My two roommates and I decided that on Hallowe'en we were going to pull a good one. My one roommate had a little Volkswagen bug.

So we approached the guys above and said, "We're going to stick the legs of a body out the front of the Volkswagen and we're going to drive all around town, and we're going to have balaclavas on because with professional women, it wouldn't look too good." And then we were going to park this thing underneath his clock, which we absolutely did.

So we asked the guys if we could borrow their ski poles and some pants. So we made stuffed legs and great big boots and we proceeded to drive around town and we were absolutely in hysterics. So we parked it underneath the light until about midnight, and then we parked it in its normal place.

It was noted in the newspaper the next week that this Volkswagen bug, and it was recognized, with three professional women...they knew who we were.

But it was just hysterical.

10. Niran Cassair – My Nephew's Wedding in Iraq

My nephew booked the club for the wedding three months earlier. They rented a big hall because they had invited a lot of people. The night before the wedding, they went to organize the hall. But the manager told them, "Sorry, but this space has been rented."

This was just after the fall of Saddam Hussein, and the new government said, "We're having a conference here, and we have booked the hall. Don't argue."

They said, "Tomorrow is the wedding! What do we do?"

"Have your wedding in the garden."

My nephew said, "No, we can't. It's February. It's the middle of winter."

He went all over, from one club to another, to all the restaurants, and no luck. They had invited 500 people.

His cousin said, "There is an electrician. He does a lot of work with us. He will help."

By now it was midnight, the day before the wedding. He went to the electrician and he said, "I have a problem, can you help me out?"

The electrician said, "Take my space, upstairs and downstairs, and use it all."

The problem was that everybody went to the other place because that's what they were told. They didn't know that the wedding was transferred. People were confused. Some just left their gifts and went home because they didn't know what was going on.

So my cousin sent his other brother there to wait for the guests and redirect them.

But there was only room for about 200 in the electrician's place. But they had invited 500 people. The others all just came and left their presents and went home.

For my own wedding, nothing much happened but my mother did not come to the church because she had too much rheumatism. So it wasn't a very eventful wedding. It was a beautiful wedding.

You ask if I married for love? I say, not for love. He saw me and then he asked for my hand. I didn't say yes right away. I left the city and kept him waiting for five days.

11. Awatif Yalda – My Father and the Mirror

My Dad was a teacher in a place called Sharafya in 1950. The first school that was built in that village was his school. He stayed there for two years, and then he went to Baghdad, the capital. There were lots of stores and lots of mirrors. My father saw a big mirror, and he saw himself and he said, "Hi, hi." He thought it was somebody there. Then he said, "That's me!" He had seen mirrors before, but never such a big one.

12. Deanna Vowels – Lemon Merengue Pie

Well, I used to cook; I don't anymore 'cause I live alone but I had two children and a husband who didn't always come home on time. However, that day I had made two beautiful lemon merengue pies, and they were sitting on the table cooling and when he came in the door, late, he looked and he said, "Oh", he said, "Those pies look so good." Then he sat down and I stood there looking at these pies.

Then I looked at him and I said, "Have you ever had an urge?"

And he said, "I dare you."

So I picked up the pie, and it went right into his face. The merengue hung off his eyebrows and off the end of his nose and I could not stop laughing. My stomach hurt so bad. The tears were rolling down my cheeks, and he looked over and said, "Can I have the rest of that pie now?"

13. Jamie Long – Suckers

There's this creek; I don't think it even had a name to it. I think a lot of people called it Long's Creek; it wasn't ours but it bordered on our property. But there's this small, slow-running creek; it wasn't more than 4 or 5 feet wide at the most. Typically it would be maybe two and a half feet. But every spring up that creek came the suckers. And they came in droves. In fact you could just about walk across their backs, there were so many of them.

It attracted all the kids in the neighbourhood to come down to catch these goofy suckers. We did everything to catch those suckers. I used the 12-gauge shotgun there to blast them out. I used snares; I could catch them with bare hands. We all did it any way we could. We gaffed them, stabbed them, hit them with clubs. You name it, because these darn suckers ate the trout eggs, and we didn't like them at all. What we'd do with them when we caught them? Absolutely nothing. We pulled these fish out. One year I got over 500; I counted them. I got over 500 and they lay on the creek bank. I betcha that soil was the best soil of any place goin' because of the suckers left there to rot. And in the early summer it reeked down there along that creek. It was foul.

So anyway, I don't know how old I was, probably ten or eleven or something. We had a set of frost-heave bumps on Highway 16, and the salesmen heading up to Prince Rupert on their route, they would come up there gunnin' their big Dodge Monacos and their big Chevrolets, those big, long boats, right? And they'd go over those bumps and they'd go flying in the air and they'd go, "Bang" and you'd hear their mufflers scraping as they went over the bumps. Of course, being the precocious little bugger I was, I get this bright idea one day, I said, "Wouldn't it be funny if I went out there and got a bunch of those suckers and put them on the other side of the bump so when they went over the bump they'll land on the fish." I thought this would be a real funny thing.

So, anyway, I went down there with a wheelbarrow and I loaded up a load of these rotten old fish, and it stunk pretty bad, but whatever, I didn't mind. So I go out there and sure enough, I ran out there real quick and I dumped all these fish across the bumps. Sure enough I watched these cars, and I'll tell you this is not a word of a lie, those big vehicles would actually skid on those fish. It was great. I was proud of myself. This was such a neat thing I'd done.

Well that was until Dad got home from camp. You know, Dad would come home from camp, usually on Saturday afternoon he'd come draggin' himself in and somehow or other I guess, maybe this is a couple of weeks after the fact. By this time, what with the summer sun, what had happened to the fish at the bumps? Well of course they had gotten pretty high. In fact, it stunk like rotten fish all around the house. My Dad comes up to me one morning and he says, "I have a bone to pick with you," he says. Of course, whenever Dad said he had a bone to pick, you knew you were in deep trouble.

Sure enough, Dad says, "You know, those fish that are on the bumps there? Did you have anything to do with that?"

"Well...maybe..."

He said, "guess what? Those fish would do great in the garden."

By this time they were rotted higher than a kite.

"Aw, but Dad, they stink so bad!"

"Right. That's why you're going to bury them in the garden."

And that's what I ended up having to do. I was pretty mad at myself after all that.

14. Fayza Massour – Father's Cousin

This is about some people who died 20 years ago. It is far in the past. There was the cousin of my father was engaged to a woman whose sight was not very good. They got married, and they used to all sleep in the hall next to each other. It was all very innocent. In the night they had no lights. The wife couldn't see very well, because it was dark, so she came and slept next to her brother-in-law, not next to her husband.

In the morning he felt her presence, and he said, "Get up, get up, it's not your space."

The family always told this story. It was always a joke.

15. Sandy Long – Horses and I Don't Get Along

This story I'm going to tell was actually published in the Province newspaper. They used to have a little program for kids to write in from different parts of the province, telling about what they were doing. It was called the Tillicum Club, and this story was published there.

This is around the time when I was 6 and Gord was 5. It was in the spring of the year and we were living at home with our parents down by Highway 16, not in sawmill camp or tie hacking camp.

And Dad decided to take us fishing at Fish Lakes. Fish Lakes are around the end of Boo Mountain off to the west at the northwest end of Decker Lake. And the distance in there was perhaps five to six miles. Dad had a couple of draught horses, Maude and Topsy, that he skidded his logs with as part of his logging operation. So Dad was ridding Maude, and Gord and I were riding Topsy. At that time, Topsy was about 27 years old and her backbone was like that of a sawhorse made out of a 2X4. So we were riding this old nag bareback, and we'd just left Highway 16, heading down the little road that goes to the present day site of Decker Lake Forest Products, and just approaching CN rail. Topsy was lollygagging along not making much progress, and Dad said, "Can't you get that horse going?"

Well, Gord knew how to get the horse going; you give it a good kick in the ribs. So he gives the horse a good kick in the ribs and plop, plop! There's two kids sittin' in the dust and Topsy walking along.

So that's how our trip started. We went on this close-to-6-mile trail ride, culminating in a shortcut because, like his son, Dad was one for taking a shortcut when he knew there was a good one, and I clearly remember Topsy walking under a big spreading pine tree with big branches and just scraping two kids right off her rear, and, "Oh, you guys gonna stay on that horse or not?"

These were big horses such that kids, sitting on the back of her, granted she had a backbone like a 2X4 but then her belly stretched out so that we were doing the splits the whole day. I think I counted that we both fell off, because we both fell off together, about 6 times. We did manage to make it to the stream. It was the spring of the year, and Gord caught a fish and I didn't, and it put me off horse riding for the rest of my life. My little 4-year-old brother caught a fish and I didn't catch a fish, and after all that agony of riding that danged horse.

So anyway, I'm not a horseman, much to the chagrin of my relatives, many of whom were fine horse people.

In fact I'll tell a little corollary to this story. Auntie Jean Reynolds was terminally ill in the Prince George hospital, and a bunch of us had gathered around her bed, and we were telling tales and laughing and joking, and I confessed to her that I would prefer to lead the horse rather than ride it, and she went "Hmph!" She was a horsewoman through and through, and she was bitterly disappointed that one of her nephews would be so gauche as to say that he didn't like to ride a horse.

Anyway, there you go, there's my horseback tale.

16. Morgan Gadd – Earl the Squirrel

This is one of those First Time stories that you don't forget. It happened when I was in Primary Two; I was about 8 years old. It was the first time that I made friends with a wild animal.

This animal came to me in the most unusual way. It was Mother's Day, late in May. My home at that time was in part of the Rocky Mountains. And in the Rocky Mountains, you know, the winter can sometimes go over into late April or May. You can still have a snowfall because you're in the mountains.

And sure enough, on Mother's Day, the second Sunday in May, I came out the door and it had snowed the night before; a big storm had blown in. I came out my door and I went down the stairs a little bit. The snow was maybe a foot deep, and I was walking down the steps to go out to the road when I noticed there was something moving in the snow just beside me.

So I brushed the snow away, and there was something in there. I got closer, and I looked, and it was alive. It was a small creature. I thought, "What could that be? Oh, it's a bat. A black bat." But no, it was daytime; it couldn't be a bat. But it was something black and small. So I looked up in the tree, and there was some kind of a nest up there. So I thought, "A bird. A small bird has fallen out of the nest from the storm."

So I brushed the snow aside a little more, and I reached down and brought it out. It was something I had never seen before. It was a baby, some kind of a newborn something.

It reminded me exactly of what had happened in my family a few days ago. Alice, our beautiful white cat, had just had six kittens. And this thing I had in my hand looked just like a baby kitten. I thought, "What is it?"

So, foolishly, I suppose, I picked it up and held it, and I brought it in to my mother. I said, "Look what I found outside."

And she said, "Oh, my gosh, what have you got?"

I said, "I don't know. What is it? What is it?"

She took it and looked at it and she said, "That's a baby black squirrel. What are we going to do with it?"

Well, Alice had just had kittens, and we thought maybe we could put this baby squirrel in with the cat, and maybe she would take it and nurse it and help it to grow up with the other kittens. Maybe she would accept it. But you know animals are sometimes picky about the young that they choose.

So we put this little squirrel down with the mother cat. The mother was lying on her side, and the baby cats were feeding, and sure enough, Alice allowed the baby black squirrel to nurse.

And because it was Mother's Day, and because my father was a newspaper reporter, he said, "We have to take a picture of this and send it up to the newspaper, and let other people in the community know." So he had a photographer come, and they took a picture of Alice with the little squirrel who I had named Earl.

They asked me, "Why did you name the squirrel, 'Earl'?"

I said, "Well, that's his name. Earl the Squirrel. It rhymes."

So they took the photo and they put in on the front page of the paper on Mother's Day.

So Earl joined the family, and he was my squirrel. He became my secret friend and pet. One thing, though, we were not allowed to let Earl out of the house. If we let him out, he would probably take off. So Earl stayed in the house. He began to grow. At first he was with the kittens, but after a while he started to grow teeth, because squirrels are rodents, and their teeth come in faster than kittens. So Alice couldn't nurse him anymore because he would bite and it was painful.

So we had to take him away from her and go to the veterinarian and get a little bottle, like a doll would have. We got this little bottle, and we put a special formula of milk from the veterinarian in it, and we were able to feed Earl with the

41

baby bottle. I would hold him and he'd feed, and gradually I became bonded with this squirrel, and I was like a father to him.

It was the first time I had a friend who came in from the wild into my home.

Earl would stay with me. He would ride on my shoulder around the house. He would sleep with me, all tucked under my neck. He would run around the house. We had a model ship above the fireplace, and he would go up there and sleep and play.

When my grandmother would come to visit, he would do the craziest thing. She would stand at the door, and she would say, "Where's that squirrel? Where's that squirrel?" and she would hold her dress down, because he used to run over and run up her stockings and roar around inside her dress. She went "Ow, ow, that squirrel, ow, ow!"

So Earl would do crazy stuff like that. But I really got to like him.

And then another first time thing came. We had to move out of that neighbourhood and go to another. And in moving, we had to take our furniture to the new house. We made a cage for Earl and we put him in there. We moved him to the other house and left him there outside in the yard while we went back for another load of furniture.

Then we came back again I went to see Earl, and he was lying in his cage. He was just lying there. He wasn't moving. "I said, 'What...what happened?'"

I went over to him and there was some blood coming out of his mouth. "What...?"

Earl was dead. He was dead. And that was the first time in my life that I experienced the death of a pet that I really loved.

I remember taking Earl out and he was just flopping, and he was dead. I was crying, of course. And then the neighbour girl, whose name was Laura, came over and said, "Do you know what happened?"

I said, "No, what happened?"

She said, "When you went back to get the other furniture, some boys in the neighbourhood came over, and they were looking at Earl in the cage. Earl was very friendly. He wanted to come out and play with them, I guess. And one of the boys reached in and took him out. And they really liked him, I guess, so the boy put Earl inside his shirt and began to ride away on his bicycle."

They stole him. They kidnapped Earl!

"They were riding their bikes along," she said, "And Earl came out of the shirt and jumped out and the boy rode over Earl with the bicycle. It broke his back and killed him. It squashed him."

And the boys felt so terrible that they picked Earl up and they brought him back and they put him inside the cage like nothing had happened. Except something really did happen, and he was dead.

So Earl had died, and I didn't know really what to do about that. I tried to find out who did it, but nobody would say. And to this day, I don't know who killed Earl. But that was the time that I lost a dear, dear friend who happened to be wild, but at the same time, he wasn't so wild to me. Earl the Squirrel.

17. Praval Dadwal – The Scooter Lesson

One funny thing that I can share with kids. I'm from India, and there's a place called Chandever, which is known for its roundabouts. We manage the traffic through roundabouts. In summer we would go there as a group and we would sit on the roundabout for hours and talk to each other and watch people go by.

One day we were sitting by the roundabout and we saw a guy who came by on a scooter and he said, "You know how to ride?" And he went past.

Then he came back around, and he said, "You know how to ride?" and he went around, and he came back, and he said, "You know how to ride?"

We said, "What is he doing? Why is he asking that? Is he trying to tease us?"

Then we heard a big bang, and we saw he was lying down in the street, so we rushed to him and asked, "What happened? You were asking us, 'Do you know how to ride?' and then you fell."

And he said, "That's why I was asking you if you knew how to ride. Where is the brake?"

18. Jennifer Lukin – Missing the Boat

Once in a while we wonder what would be like if we weren't here, or how life would go. This story goes back quite a few generations to my great-grandparents, who lived in England. My great-grandfather was a cobbler, with not a lot of money, but he had saved up some money to go on a trip to the US with my great-grandmother and their three daughters. They had bought tickets for this big boat to ride. Everyone was really excited, but as they got closer to that journey the business was starting to go downhill, so he thought, "I'll sell my ticket and the family can still go, and everything will be fine."

My great-grandmother said, "No, I don't want to go without you. I want us to all be together."

He insisted up until the day before the journey. But then he said, "Okay, if I can sell the tickets, we'll all stay behind and we'll save the money."

Well, sure enough, he did find someone to buy those tickets, and the name on the tickets was, "Titanic."

So if history had been just a little bit different, my parents wouldn't be here. I wouldn't be here, my children wouldn't be here, and so on.

And that's something to think about.

19. Awatif Yalda– My Father's Roommate

This story happened in 1945, before I was born, close to Mosul at Al Qosh. People were coming from the outskirts of Al Qosh. They didn't have cars in those days, and they would come on donkeys or mules.

My father was a tailor, and it used to take him about a day to go from Al Qosh to Mosul, so he would usually stay overnight there.

An older woman came to Al Qosh from our original village. She used to make quilts and blankets to sell. My father's parents owned a pension, or hotel. It was rooms all around a central courtyard. They told her, "Stay with us because our son is not coming home, and you can spend the night in a place where you know the people. You can use his room."

But my father came home that night, very late. It was dark, and he couldn't see. He went to his room and didn't know that the woman was there, and he just took his blanket and threw it on the bed over top of her, and climbed onto the bed.

She started screaming. "Oh! There's a man! There's a man!" My father didn't know what happened.

20. Jamie Long – Riding Lesson by Truck

Mother of course was the piano teacher and everybody would come out to the Long establishment to get their musical training and their artistic merits honed by Mrs. Long the piano teacher.

So anyway, it happened to be a Saturday, and Mrs. Gelz, who was quite a fussy woman in a lot of ways and loved her kids a lot, had come out with her kids, Des and Christine. Christine being a year younger than me. I didn't really have a crush on her, but I liked her well enough, and Mrs. Gelz was fine, and Des Gelz was older than me. But he was having his lesson, and I said to Christine, "Would you like to go out for a horseback ride?"

Now, these aren't normal horses, you understand. These are Clydesdale and Morgan mixed, so these are big horses with great big monstrous Clydesdale hooves to them. We had Maude and Star. What happened that Maude and Topsy were a team, and then Topsy died, and we ended up replacing Topsy with Star. And what happened with Star was that she had been in a pickup truck accident – it rolled backwards down a hill and turned over, with her in the back – and she was deathly afraid of trucks.

So, anyway, this was in the wintertime, with big snowbanks, Christine and I passed Dick Carroll Hill and were heading out towards the swimming hole. Then we decided it was time to get back because it was getting close to her lesson, so we started to gallop along the road.

Then we hear this truck coming over the hill up above the swimming hole, and we hear him applying the Jake brake as he comes down the hill.

I say to Christine, "Hang onto your britches and head her for the driveway, because I tell you what. If that transport truck comes past here, Star's gonna go gunnin' into the ditch with all that snow and pull you with her. So come on, let's go. Head her for the yard."

So anyway I'm laughing myself silly because she's stricken. Her face is in a panic. And I'm riding old Maude, and I've been riding Maude since I was six years old, and I really know how to ride.

So I come thundering into the driveway, and these are the big Clydesdale feet, and you can imagine, it was a fresh snowfall, and quite dry, and it was all up in plumes, and I come thundering in. Needless to say, Mrs. Gelz is sitting at the kitchen table and looks out to see me come galloping in the yard pell-mell and of course her darling daughter is thundering behind on Star with the transport truck right behind Star.

Oh, my gosh, you can imagine Mrs. Gelz's eyes were like saucers. Meanwhile I come in laughing myself silly, and Christine comes flying in, Star's just a gunnin' to get in the gate, because she was scared of that transport truck. Sure enough, down goes Christine into that morass of thundering hooves and flying snow and ice and whatever.

Needless to say, I'm busting my gut laughing.

Out the door comes Mrs. Gelz crying, "My baby, my baby!"

Of course, Christine wasn't hurt. Those horses were so used to us kids falling off around them. But Mrs. Gelz was absolutely beside herself. She thought for sure that Christine was dead.

It was great.

21. Ana Dadwal – Colours

My grandma and a couple of best friends used to have lots of fun, playing tag, flying kites, and doing all sorts of things. But one festival and one particular day they used to wait for every year was a very famous festival in India called Holi, where people play with colours, water guns, water balloons and have lots and lots of fun.

The day before Holi my grandmother and her friends were planning their shopping list of some colours, some water balloons and everything they were going to need. And that day at around 6 pm they decided to make another list: of people they wanted to get and splash with colour.

They finished the list, but there was just one thing left. It was a question mark. My grandma's friends asked my grandma, "What is this question mark for? What are we going to use it for?"

She said, "It's a surprise. Today we are going to go and buy a special kit of colours, which if you put it on somebody's face or anywhere else, it stays on there almost permanently, and takes time to get off."

They went out and bought those colours.

It was morning, and everybody was getting ready, because around noon the festival was going to begin. They were planning out where they were going to throw the water balloons from and everything. But my grandma's friend asked her. "Oh, you never told us what the special colours are for, and whom you are going to use them on."

She said, "I have a neighbour, and he's a really grouchy man who never laughs and never smiles and never comes out to play. We need to get him coloured. Nobody ever saw him have fun or play anything in many years."

It was a pretty good idea, except the way my grandma said it. She was the bossy sort, kind of rude at that age. So she screamed and screamed until everybody agreed with what she said. Her friends were so scared of her at that moment that their reply came out like a squeak. "Yes, yes, we understand. Yes, yes, we're going to do what you say. Yes, yes, yes, yes."

They got the colours and gathered a couple of more friends.

The buildings at that time used to be two or three stories high. They gathered everything up, got a huge ladder and climbed up on the roof. At that time there used to be a water tank on the roof that was used to give water to the showers. I am guessing that some of you know what's going to happen. If you don't know, I'm going to tell it to you.

Well, they opened the tank and threw all those colours in and everything else they could find. They stirred it all up and closed it.

Then they came downstairs and hid, peering out the window.

Guess what? About a half an hour later the neighbour came in, took a shower, got dressed, looked himself in the mirror and screamed as loud as he could, because he was all coloured up.

My grandma's friends were laughing like crazy, but my grandma knew that if he heard them, he would be very, very mad. She was trying to calm them down. "Shh, shh, be quiet, he's going to hear us."

But it was too late. They got caught. He called all their parents. They got scolded, got a nice beating and got grounded for a week. But it was okay. It was the best day they ever had.

22. Wanda Green – Lobster Dinners

My husband and his friends rented a cottage in Constance Bay, just outside of Ottawa, and we used to laugh that it had cold and cold running water and was furnished in Early Depression. But we would have these parties. One week it might be Enrico Fermi baked bean night, or it might be roast beef night, but we decided one year we were going to have a lobster party.

We wanted live lobster, so we researched it and found there was a company back east that would ship them in. My husband worked for the airline. So they would ship them in live, and they'd go out to the airport and pick them up and bring them back to the cottage. We had a huge iron pot; I think they used to make lye in it, but it was many, many years old. The fellas built this huge campfire, and it was all encased with stone that they had found on the beach and it was quite the thing. My husband had rigged up this pole – don't know what else to call it – to hang this pot on. So they get the fire going and the water ready to boil, and then they'd go out to the airport and pick up these lobsters.

The first year we were having this we decided there was no way we could afford to buy lobster for everybody, so we better sell tickets. So we sold tickets for the lobster party, and the lobster we received was pound and a half, pound and three quarters. The price of a ticket was for a pound of lobster, so we were kind of out of pocket that first year, and we said, "Oh, we won't let this happen again."

The next year we did the same thing. I was never very good with math, and my husband had left me in charge. Big mistake.

But we would set up a tent. The first couple of years we had the party, it rained. But rain or shine we had this lobster party and everybody was quite happy under the canvas. Not a tent, a canopy. They rigged up this canopy with tarps that you would use to cover your car or cover your back yard.

So they were a lot of fun back in the day when drinking and driving was not such a critical factor as it is today. To this day we don't know how we ended up with no accidents, no fights, no broken bottles, no driving impairment charges. We were lucky, when you think about a hundred and ten people, that's probably one couple per car. They didn't even car share at that time. So you're talking maybe 50 vehicles, and we never had a problem. But we sure had some good parties.

23. Roslyn Simon – Chores on the Chicken Farm

Growing up in Trinidad, we lived on a hill and my father had a poultry farm, which was mass production because our poultry farm sold chickens. We had help who came to look after the poultry, but if they did not arrive by 6 o'clock in the morning to feed these chickens, whether I was dressed in my uniform and ought to go to school, I had to change and go make sure those chickens were taken care of.

The one thing I learned about livestock and I'll always say it's the best thing for raising children is having a farm, because animals are unforgiving. If they used to being fed at 6 am, you do not go at 6:02 or 6:05 because they'll start picking at you, literally they attack you because I have been pecked. This is one of the reasons I had to learn how to debeak chickens. You know, you burn the beaks so that they don't pick at each other because they pick at you and pick at each other if they were not fed on time. It was a quite an interesting experience.

I also learn how to kill chickens, and to put them in hot water and pluck them and degut them.

But I have an allergy to this day to poultry. I don't eat it, I don't touch it, and of course I can't have dung or anything around because I'm allergic to feathers as well. But here it is, I was raised on it. We didn't know I had an allergy until I was going to school in New York and I ended up with a very bad ear infection. I had this ear infection all my life. As a child growing up I had the best specialist that looked after me, but it was always there. It's when they did the allergy test in New York that the doctors at Columbia Presbyterian discovered that I had an allergy to poultry.

24. Joanne – My Daughter's Music Lessons.

When my daughter was 5 years old, I decided that she should take music lessons and learn to play properly, because I play by ear, and I couldn't teach her. And since we had a music teacher living right behind us it was easy for her to get to her music lessons.

Every morning at 8 o'clock I had her practise for half an hour before going to school. And she hated every minute of it. She didn't get my genes because she was adopted. Well, she'd sit down to the piano, and she would kick the piano, she would cry and she'd run to the bathroom. And after three years of this nonsense I thought, "Why am I doing this?" She is athletic so I thought I'd quit the piano lessons and buy her sports equipment. Best thing I ever did.

3. Breaking Loose

1. Deanna Vowels – Singing

When I first lived with my dad and my stepmother, my dad used to wake me up at night when they had company, to perform, to sing for them.

But when I was 9, my stepbrother was born and of course he was the first child in that marriage. One time I heard my Dad say, "Yes, I'm glad it was a boy and not another girl like her." That was the first insult I heard as a child.

The second one was from my stepmother saying, "Why are you looking in a mirror? You are homely."

The third one was: "Why are you singing? You're flat."

And for some reason, I said to myself, – I come from Hungarian stock and that must have been a catalyst to make me say it – "You're not gonna say that about me. I'm gonna be pretty. I'm gonna sing. No one is gonna stop me."

I sang all through school. Then I got married and had 2 children of my own. My husband wouldn't let me sing. If we were out somewhere and I sang, he'd walk out of the room. But I wasn't about to listen to anybody who told me that I couldn't do what I wanted to do, which was sing.

I belonged to a group called the Western Word Processing Association, and we used to have our meetings at the Georgia Hotel downtown. We were having our meeting, and I had to go downstairs to find a washroom, and I heard this music. I thought, "I have to peek in there and see what that's all about."

So I looked in and there in front of me was a fellow that worked in the mailroom where I worked, and he was playing the drums. And so I thought, "Oh, they must take a break sometime, I'll wait and see what happens."

He had seen me, and we waved. I waited, and they took their break, and we said. "Hello."

I sat down and I said, "I didn't know you played the drums," And he said, "Oh, yeah, I've been playing for so long." I said, "I sing."

He said, "Really? We happen to have an Open Mic on Tuesdays. Why don't you come down?"

Well, I had never really sung in public before. The mic shook in my hand, my knees knocked together, and I stood there steadfast, because this goes along with everything I said. I was determined to sing because music was in my soul. I loved music and I loved to perform. I'm a real diva, I guess.

So I went down to the Open Mic and the fella that ran it was a Scotsman who had the gig through the week all the time, but he had this Open Mic on the Tuesday. Anyone could come and perform, but he wasn't really fond of women. He was more or less, you know, a chauvinist, but a good entertainer, and he would call the men up and he'd give them three songs to sing, and if he did deign to call up a woman, he'd let her sing one song.

It was very difficult for me at first, because I was so nervous, because it was an audience in front of me and they were really close, and you could look right at them. But I persevered, and I'd go down and I think a couple of times he gave me two songs to sing, so you know, it worked out for me.

I went on a tour through Europe. That meant that there was a tour guide who did all the talking, and we got ourselves to England, and then we flew from England to Greece and got on the bus the next morning and away we went.

Of course the tour guides are going on about this and that, it was all very nice because you're learning a bunch of stuff, but at one point on the second day towards the end of that day when we were going to be getting to our hotel, I went up to the front of the bus, and said, "Excuse me, it's my turn," took the microphone and sang them a song. That night, when we did finally go out for dinner, we were all sitting at various little spots around this restaurant and I hear this funny noise, and I'm thinking "what's going on?" and the next thing I know in front of me is a bowl full of drachmas, the money to "sing for your supper." Which was kind of cute.

So all through the tour, which was like 19 cities in 20 days, every once in a while they'd say, "Deanna, sing us a song."

I even got emails later on from people from all over from Australia, Chile, Mexico and places in the States, everything. I got emails saying, "Are you still singing?"

It was really a boost for me, after people telling me, "you can't sing," to be entertaining people. And that's what I love to do the most is entertain.

2. Jack Lillico – Hitchhiking in Kilts

I wanted to go to a magic convention, the Pacific Coast Association of Magicians, and I didn't have transportation at that time, so Rolf Blackstead and I decided we were going to hitchhike, and wear kilts. But then Rolf backed out of the trip.

So I went to my job that I had before the trip, it was Knighton's Music Store, opposite the Bay on Seymour Street. We were making guitars and mandolins. We got talking over lunch, and two of the fellas there belonged to the Seaforth Highlanders Cadets, and they were pretty high up, I can't remember the names of their positions, but anyway we discussed the fact and decided to hitchhike down to the convention. They could get the kilts for us.

We started off; somebody drove us to Bellingham, and I don't remember who, but we hitchhiked down from there, and we got a ride into Oregon and the guy dropped us off about 1 in the morning in the middle of the mountains. So we set a fire on the side of the road and stood around with our kilts held out, getting warm. We didn't have any gear or tent or anything, because we were going to stay in hotels.

But that's how that happened. Some guy just baled us off.

You know traffic wasn't that bad. Truckers were running a lot. We rode in many trucks because there was room for that, for three of us.

So then we hitchhiked down to Watsonville, a hundred miles south of San Francisco, and stayed at my aunt's place the second night. I don't remember exactly maybe it was the third night, but anyway we arrived in Los Angeles and we took a streetcar to Pershing Square, which was in the centre of old Los Angeles. We ran into some guy there who thought we were from the Greek Army because they have similar outfits.

It was a rundown area of town, but we went to the hotel, and the convention was there, and Bergen was there, too, but I didn't see him.

We lasted at the convention for one day, and it continued for three days, but somebody gave us passes to MGM and the next morning we went over to MGM and met Spencer Tracey, Katherine Hepburn, Mickey Rooney, Katherine Grayson and Gene Kelly. Gene Kelley was a guy who was the same off the screen as on the screen, a real nice guy. I've got all their signatures at home.

The next morning we were late to Paramount, and they wouldn't let us in. We were half and hour late.

People really treated us well. I think I sold my boat for 250 bucks, and that was my travelling money, and after three weeks I came back with $65. So you can imagine that everybody really...you know, we'd go to a café, and the beer would be set up for us and that sort of thing.

I also wanted to go to Disneyland because I wanted to be an apprentice cartoonist because I was cartooning in those days. But we were riding on a streetcar about two weeks into the trip and one of the guys was crying.

I said, "What's wrong with you?"

He says, "Well, I'm homesick."

So we went immediately, bypassed Disney, and hitchhiked up to San Francisco, where somebody gave us a couple of tickets for a stage play with Edmund Gwynn or something. After the stage play there was a woman standing in the lobby that came over to us and said she wanted to buy our Glengarry hats. Well, we couldn't sell the hats, so we agreed with her to get a hat sent to her when we got home.

She owned the Regal Pale Beer Company, and we went over for lunch there the next morning, and after lunch she said, "Where are you going?"

I said, "We're going to hitchhike to Oakland, to the Army Air Base and hitchhike a plane up to Seattle. Mind you, we drank a lot of beer in the beer plant. But anyway she supplied a limousine and a driver who drove us over to Oakland, and within ten minutes we were on a plane to Seattle, my first ride in a plane.

Then we hitchhiked home.

3. Marg Kennet – Life With Father.

Yes, life with Father was really something else. I suppose a lot of girls would have rebelled, but I just didn't have the guts. But trouble really started rearing its ugly head when I was a teenager. Just to give you an idea how strict and weird Father was; he didn't want me to get hurt. So I wasn't allowed to ride a bike. And of course this just devastated me. All my friends had bikes, and so it wasn't till about age 13 or 14 I guess that my friends taught me how to rid a bike.

So I'm not a very good bike rider as an adult. That was pretty scary.

I had quite a few friends while I was in Elementary School, but going into high school I couldn't do the things they could do. I wasn't allowed to go to dances. Nooo; I might get into trouble. I wasn't allowed to join any of the teens. Nooo, because I might get into trouble. So my life was just plain bad. Mum was a very quiet, submissive person and nobody was going to overrule Father, right.

It got to the point where I was about to go to university in 1962. It was UVic, which at the time was Victoria College. I went there for the first two years.

It was really something. I had gone to UVic for two years. I was twenty by that time, and I'm getting the heck out of Dodge.

This is not going to go on any longer. So I made up this story. I was in Political Science and Psychology.

I said to Father, "If I want to major in Political Science, I have to go to UBC, because Vic College doesn't have the variety of courses and I just need to do this." I have no idea of how he let me go. I guess maybe he thought the inevitable was going to happen some time.

Anyway, ah, boy. I couldn't believe it. That was the first year that Totem Park Residence opened. And life began at almost 21. It was just a miracle that I didn't really get into a lot of trouble. Because I was this retiring little girl all through High School, and then at university at UBC I thought, "Yeah, there's fun to be had here." So I just had one good time. Managed to pass my courses, but I was working at the Bay as well, and I was shoving toast in the toaster at Residence, and then dances every Friday night and all sorts of good fun.

And then in 4th year I had this horrible Political Science prof who was totally boring. I had him for two courses and he said after midterm in the fall, "Anybody who passes and does well on the midterm, I'm not going to have you write the final."

I thought, "Yes!"

So I never went to another class again. As did quite a few of my classmates.

And then, come April, the Powers That Be said, "Professor laPonte, you can't do that."

So I did not get my BA because I had to concentrate on my other four courses, right? I could not pick up nine months of the course. So I ended up having to take Philosophy 100 by correspondence after I got out of university.

4. Dorothea Lowndes – Marrying an Englishman

I was going to a Catholic school, a private school, an incredible effort my father had to make when he had 5 kids to pay for. I was going to school and I used to see this hotel, and it was a bunch of English guys there and I remember this fellow waving his hand, motioning, "Come."

I was with my friends. "It's you he's talking to."

"Talking to me? No he's just waving his hand." It was eight o'clock in the morning, and school would start, so I said "No, no, I'm not paying attention to that. I'm not a dog, 'Come,' so I walked away and I went to school.

I went to the club in the nighttime with my oldest sister, and he was outside the club, and he wanted to get my attention, and I said, "He doesn't understand."

So he crossed the road and he came and told me who he was, and could I help him with his Portuguese.

I said, "How?"

And he said, "I want to buy some handkerchiefs. I went to the store, and I know the word for 'handkerchief' in Portuguese, it's 'linsol,' isn't it?"

So I burst out laughing. I said, "Linsol?"

He said, "Yeah, but what I don't understand was why you have to get a big sheet and cut in small pieces to make handkerchief."

I said, "The word for 'handkerchief' is 'lenço,' so when you ask for linsol, the lady thought you wanted a sheet. That's why she said, "You want twelve? You in a hotel?"

I said, "You have to use your hands, Brazilians use their hands for everything, you know, it's to clean your nose."

Anyway, we start talking once in a while, and there was a girlfriend of mine that spoke better English than I did, and she said, "Oh, we're going to the movies."

I said, "Oh, good."

"I'm going with him."

"Terrific."

Anyway, he said, "No, no, I want her to come and you to translate."

And she said, "I'm coming because you can't speak English."

My not-yet husband said, "That's okay, we're not going to be talking very much. We're going to a movie."

I lost a friend, that's for sure.

So that's how we started. And all that lasted only seven months, and he was going back to England, and I went back to England with him.

5. Joanne Harris – My Escape

I was born in January 1929 in northern Saskatchewan. It was near Melfort and when my mother was in labour my Dad had to travel to Melfort with a team of horses to get a doctor to help her. I was the youngest of 8 children.

My oldest sister was married when I was 6 years old. My brother told me we thought it was good riddance because she was my mother's right-hand man. She was the disciplinarian.

Life went along and my parents had a little post office and a small grocery store in a place called Lenville. I thought, "This is quite dull, living here. I'm gonna be either doomed to spinsterhood or marry a local yokel like my sisters, and that isn't for me."

My older brothers and sisters scattered because there was nothing really to keep them around. Not all of them, because my sisters were married to the local yokels. This wasn't going to happen to me. When they were all leaving home, I was on my own with my ageing parents and I was determined to leave home too. And I thought I would like to do secretarial work. I didn't know what was out there to do. When you're brought up in an isolated area, you don't know. But I knew that there was such a thing as being a steno or a secretary.

But my father was strict, and he wouldn't let me go. He never gave me a reason; he just wanted to hang on to me. I tried to persuade them to send me to business college. No, that wasn't gonna happen.

So I appealed to my brother, who was a veteran during the war, and he asked my parents whether I could go to Winnipeg to go to business college, and he would pay my tuition. Still "No."

So I had to take the matter into my own hands. I had to escape custody. I was 17,

So I'm planning my escape. I had a neighbour who took an interest in me, and she bought a suitcase and I kept taking bits and pieces over to her. I would climb out the window of our house at the back and I would tell her where I would leave my little bundle, and she would pack my suitcase.

It was September 26, 1946 that I made my escape. We had a train going past our little village every day and it always stopped because they would leave a small mailbag or pick up water. I thought, "I'm just gonna get on that train on September 26. Which I did. My neighbor left the suitcase on the platform of the station. We had no station agent.

I got on that train and apparently my mother saw me getting on the train. I had long, cascading hair. Can you picture that? And she saw me getting on that train. I had left a note for them in the post office.

My brother was looking out for me from a distance. He was going to McGill University at that time. As I mentioned, he was a veteran. He warned me not to accept favours from strangers. Now, when did I know when to apply that warning at age 17? I didn't know what he was talking about.

Anyway, I'm travelling from Melfort, and I had to get a ticket at the station agent to go to Winnipeg. The reason I was going to Winnipeg was because I knew a teacher there who was teaching shorthand at Success Business College.

I got on this train, travelling to Winnipeg. I had to change trains in Lannigan, and being a hick you might say, I had to really keep my wits about me. I got on the train in Lannigan, and because it was late in the season, there was hardly anybody on this train.

The porter was black. I had never seen a black person in my life. There was no television when I was growing up. I was quite fascinated by this chocolate man. He asked my where I was going, and struck up a conversation with me, and I told him what I was up to. And he said, "Are you going to be having a sleeping berth?"

And I said, "No, I'm going to be sitting up."

And he said, "Well the train is quite empty. I will let you have a berth for nothing, and you can save the money for schoolbooks."

So I thought, "Yeah, that's nice of him."

It was an upper berth, and the way my mind worked, I wasn't going to take off my clothes when going to bed, because I thought I wouldn't have time when we arrived in Winnipeg to get dressed again. So I just lay on this upper berth.

After a little while the curtain on this upper berth was moving, and this porter was talking to me. He said, "Would you like me to read you a bedtime story?"

And I said, "Oh, no, thank you."

So he went away, and I thought. "What a funny thing for him to want to do."

That was it. Nothing happened. But the results could have been disastrous.

My daughter likes that story.

6. Jamie Long – Mum's New Job.

I think the year was 1938, could be 1939, but it was just before the war broke out, and Mum had just finished Normal School training in Victoria. Here she was, a young girl who had spent a lot of her life trying to please her mother, getting her ARTC piano teaching degree and getting good marks in school. She had many aunts and uncles and she was an only child. A very sheltered life. I think her move to accept a job in a small rural school in Northern B.C. was to get away from the aunts, the uncles and her Mum.

Anyway she accepted this job to teach in Palling, which is a small farming community outside of Burns Lake, 650 miles north of Vancouver.

So Mum dutifully gets her things together and heads out on the CN rail, disembarks in Jasper and transfers to get the line out to Burns Lake. When she got to Burns Lake she was met by the School Inspector. He showed up with a bouquet of flowers and said, "Good day, Miss Seely. Welcome to Burns Lake. I'm sorry to tell you that your school burned to the ground last night."

Needless to say, Mum was flabbergasted at this.

"But they've arranged that you'll teach school in Alvin Long's house, where you'll be billeted. They have a large front room and they have a piano." When my Mum heard that there was a piano she perked up and didn't feel so bad.

So they jumped into the Inspector's Model A and drove seven miles out to Palling to the Long's farm and Mum's new job. Then they drove up into the community, farms and rolling fields in mainly hay and clover. And as they came over the crest of Faisal's hill, they could look out, and there was the Long household, in a beautiful location with Merril creek running right beside the house, and there was this huge cliff overlooking the back of the property. And up on that hillside they could see a lone rider coming down out of the timber.

As they proceed up this rough road to the Long establishment, the rider comes down to open the gate for the Model A. As he got closer, Mum could see that there was a quarter of moose tied behind the saddle, and a brace of grouse hung over the saddle horn. And sitting in the saddle was this young gentleman with a black cowboy hat on. Not a bad looking guy with kind of a twinkle in his eye. He reached down and opened up the gate without getting off his horse and pulled it back so that they could drive up to the house.

Bill says, "Miss Seely, I'd like to introduce you to Art, one of Alvin Long's younger boys."

The gentleman tipped his hat to her and said, "Good afternoon, Miss Seely."

And of course, since he had brought a gift to the family household, the son was invited to join them for dinner that night. And as he took his place across the table, Art winked at the new schoolteacher.

And that was how my Mum met my Dad.

7. Brenda Casey – Firsts

I was growing up in Winnipeg, and I was lucky enough to be there when we had our centennial. I was only 14 years old, and I started working for the Centennial Corporation on a part-time basis. I typed really quickly. My mother taught me how to type at a young age. I was typing 80 or 90 words a minute on one of these old Underwood typewriters. So I got this job with the Centennial Corporation, and they had planned a conference for young people. One of the subjects of the conference was, "Is the Canadian Indian a Second Class Citizen?"

Now, I think you know from other stories that I've told that my background is purely Jewish. Until I was 12, I didn't know there was anyone who wasn't Jewish, I just thought they were different kinds of Jewish people.

By the time I was 14 I was a little more aware of that, but by the time I was 15 the Centennial Corporation had this event for the summer. They put me in charge of moderating this discussion group, which was about whether the Canadian Indian was a second-class citizen.

So I come into this room and there's maybe 20 other kids in there. All young people, and all of them are Indian, except for one guy who actually was a First Nations boy, but he looked white. And because he looked white, he was quite arrogant towards all the other folks in the room.

They all went to residential school in Winnipeg. Not knowing anything about residential schools, because like I said, I'd been Jewish for a long time, I didn't know what was going on at residential schools and this was never discussed.

The discussion group was quite a heated one, talking about what it felt like to be an Indian kid in a white society, and coming out of the residential school and meeting white people, and they didn't know too many white people, and so I was one of the few white people that they knew.

I told them about being Jewish, because they'd never met anyone who was Jewish, and they told me what it was like to be mixed race or Indian; some of them were Metis, some of them were pure First Nations.

They talked to me about their history, and I actually got an incredibly good education from them around the French influence in their lives. I became quite close friends with a boy that was in that group. A fellow named Robert Houle, who is one of the top Canadian First Nations artists now, and he actually curated the First Nations segment in the National Gallery.

Anyhow, Bob and I became friends, and I got to know this young man who looked white, who was named Leonard. And Bob's sister was there, and I met a number of his friends. We became friends over the years.

I was invited to the residential school to come to a school dance and that sort of thing. It was a good experience, but nothing around the issues of residential schools was ever imparted to me until a number of years later.

One thing I really learned was that I didn't like this boy, Leonard. I really didn't like him. Bob and I were talking about him one day, because he came to a dinner that we had, and Bob said, "Well, you don't like him because he's Indian."

I said, "I don't like him because he's an idiot." It was the first time in my life that I'd said I didn't like somebody, and they were a person of colour. And it made it clear to me that there are people who are white, who are black, who are green, who are yellow, any colour, and there are great people and there are not-so-great-people, and it doesn't matter what colour they are, they can just be not great people.

And it was a new piece of learning for me as a youngster. I was about 16 at the time. And it had nothing to do with his race, religion or colour, but I didn't like him.

That was very new to me.

8. Brenda Casey – Another First

The other first was that Bob, the young man that was First Nations, invited me to his freshman coming out, I guess it was called. He was the first First Nations person at the University

64

of Manitoba, he and his sister, actually. There was a special event that was held in our concert hall in Winnipeg, and I got invited to be his date.

My mother and father were very anxious about that. They'd never had any of their daughters dating someone who wasn't Jewish. Let alone someone who wasn't Caucasian. Let alone someone who was First Nations.

I remember having the discussion with them, and saying, "I could sneak out, or I could have him come and pick me up and we'd go open and aboveboard."

My father was not keen. My mother was much more open-minded about it, which surprised me. So they let it happen, and when Bob came to pick me up, he came with his friend, who was going to pick up his date, and his friend was from Trinidad. My mother's eyes went in and out of her head twice.

But we went to this wonderful event and then we came back to my house, and my mother had prepared some food for us. My room was in the lower level of my house. In Winnipeg you have basements in every house, so there was a downstairs area that was pretty separated from the rest of the house, and she let us be downstairs. And we danced, and it was a lovely evening, but it was quite an education for me and for my parents, because that began a process of me dating fellows who were not the people my parents would have chosen.

In general, I was surprised that my mother would stand up for me to my father. I was surprised that my father was the one who didn't want me to date someone who wasn't Jewish. As I said earlier, my mother was the more prejudicial of the two.

And then how she – I'm not sure if she relaxed, – she just sucked it up and let it happen and my father as well. Neither of them were ever punitive with me about it, or judgmental or critical. It surprised me. That was one of the things that surprised me about them.

Although, when it came to marrying someone who wasn't Jewish, that was another story, but they didn't really worry about it too much.

And when I was in Israel, I was dating Jewish guys, I was dating a Lebanese guy, I was dating a Palestinian guy, it didn't worry me to think about doing that. I dated fellas from different races, and religions and colours, and it never concerned me but I think it would have influenced me greatly if this first experience hadn't ended up being as amenable as it ended up being.

4. Travel

1. Maggie Gooderham – Kenya and Tyrone Power

When I first arrived in Kenya, they had a plague of huge grasshoppers, and I thought, "Oh, I can't live here." One morning when I went into work, one of them says to me, "You have a visitor in your office, Miss Fitzgerald."

I went in and couldn't see anyone. And they were all laughing away. I looked around, and there was a huge grasshopper on my desk. I went, "Ooh, take it away," and they all laughed and said it was so funny. It's one thing I remember. They sure had a sense of humour. The plague lasted about two weeks, and then it went away.

I was working for a safari outfit. I sent them all on their way, these lovely safaris. I went on a couple of little ones, but none of these glamorous ones.

I had a friend there who was the American Consul's wife. They had to entertain all the Americans that came in. And one day she said to me that there was this film crew coming through. She said, "Would you like to go and visit? Tyrone Power is coming." So he came in and he took my hand, and said, "Good evening, Miss Fitzgerald." He was so handsome. That was a fun evening, seeing this gorgeous man, which he was, of course.

2. Jack Lillico – Model T Oven

In 1973 I decided to go on a sailing trip with my Model T and a buddy. So we went up the coast on the ferry to Prince Rupert and I sold a bunch of stuff there, and then I headed east to Prince George. Along the way I said to my buddy, "I read in the Model T Magazine where a guy cooked a roast on the head of his motor."

"Well," he says, "We can't eat a roast."

I said, "I'm only telling you. I'm not suggesting we do it."

About twenty minutes later we were coming into Terrace. He says, "Why don't we try some steaks?"

So we went in and bought two cookie pans and I naturally had some baling wire on the car, and we got some paper plates and steaks and potato salad and tin foil and seasoned salt. We wrapped it up and put it on the manifold. It was a flathead motor with the spark plugs on top, so the manifold ran under, and in about twenty minutes, wow, it smelled like Hi's Steakhouse coming out.

It started to rain, and I said, "Gee, I gotta get some gas."

So we go down this road to this little place near Terrace. By the time we turned the steaks over and drove down we got to a gas station and when we drove in you had to go into about two or three inches of water and the kid came out and never said a thing.

I said, "Fill it up." And he filled it up and then when he was making the change I said, "Don't check the oil, because you won't know how to do that."

So, he was making change, and we stood on each side of the T and we had our plates and we ate right there. It was really good. You know the smell of Hi's Steak House.

He looked like a dumb guy. He never asked any questions.

Pretty soon the whole family – the father and the mother and two or three kids – were peering out the window. It was a kind of a general store and gas station. They never came out, and we drove off. I guess they figured we came out of the sky. It was a peculiar experience.

When I got to Prince George, the rear end gave out, but I had all my parts and my tools. It took me two days to rebuild the rear end, and we carried on back to Vancouver, about 1500 miles.

3. Judith McBride – Travelling Through Russia

I was officially born in England, according to mom and dad. My dad worked for British Rail his entire life and mom was a stay-at-home mom until I was 5. When I was 13, I met my first husband and he was 14. We were 19 & 20 when we got married and when I was 20, in 1971, we decided we would travel overland from England to Australia. So that's what we did.

Our original choice was to go on the Orient Express but there was a big cholera outbreak in Turkey and so we had to bypass Turkey. We took the boat to Holland from England and then we got on a train that went through Holland and Germany and at that point it was East and West Berlin. So we went through from West Berlin to East Berlin through Poland to Moscow.

That was very interesting trip. I was scared stiff the whole time. It was my first trip out of England and I was 20 years old. When we got on the train and we had booked little sleepers. It was a three-day train trip, and the conductor or whatever he was would not let us sleep in the same room because he did not believe we were married. And we had to find a Dutch couple who spoke English, tell them in English and they could translate to him that we were married and we were allowed to actually sleep together in the same train carriage.

When we got to the outskirts of Moscow, it's one of my favourite stories. We bought food and stuff like that. They stopped the train in the middle of the night and they came through to look at our passports and stamped them all and said, "Have you got fruit and vegetables?"

We said, "Oh yes. We got an orange and tomatoes and an apple."

He said, "Eet is forbeeden. Eat now."

It was 4 in the morning and we actually started eating this fruit and vegetables. We were so scared.

Anyway we got to Moscow and it was the anniversary of the Russian Revolution. Good planning on our part. So they met us at the station. They took us to the hotel, which was full of Italian communists who were there celebrating the Russian Revolution, and us. I am sure there were other people there but that's what it seemed like. I didn't sleep a wink all night because they were moving all the big tanks through and all the big huge guns and all that stuff that was going rumble, rumble, rumble. And I was convinced they were going to declare World War III, and I was going to be stuck in Moscow.

Which did not happen of course. So we spent one night there, and they changed money for us. They gave us a coupon to go to a specific restaurant where we could eat and the food was just horrendous. Then we went back to the hotel where I didn't sleep all night.

The next morning, they came and got us 5 hours before the train was leaving because we had to clear the streets for the big parade thing. It's the first time I've ever seen guns or anything. I came from England where, you know, the police don't have them. So they stopped us everywhere with all these guns. It was pretty, pretty scary.

We got to the station and got on the train for a 5-day train journey down through Georgia, through Armenia. The most friendly people I ever met in my entire journey from England to Australia were in Russia. We never spent a single penny on the train. Every time we tried, we couldn't. When the train stopped, they said "Oh look, they've got ice cream!" and they'd be there with like 10 ice cream cones for us.

They got somebody from way down from the other end of the carriage who spoke English to come. We never had minute to ourselves in the 5-day journey. My ex-husband looked like Paul McCartney, so they just kept wanting him to sing Beatles songs. It was just the most amazing journey. Very frightening, they had a guy that used to bring tea around that was always coming in, sitting and listening. And we thought, "Oh is this KGB stuff? Are we actually gonna get out of Moscow? Or are we gonna get out of Russia?"

When we got to the border to go in to Iran, it was not a great place to go; the Shah was still there. So it really wasn't the place to go. So there was my husband, myself and a girl from Switzerland and everybody else got off and they left us to sleep on train all night. In the morning these 3 men came on and we had to empty all our luggage. We had tiny luggage because we were backpacking.

They went through everything. They went to every seam on every piece of clothing we had. They emptied everything. They found my birth control pills and went, "What's this? What's this?" And of course we didn't speak anything other than English.

But this Swiss girl spoke English and German. And one of the guys spoke German so we would tell her to translate to him and they said, "Do you have money?" And of course we hadn't spent any money because these people had bought us everything.

So we said "Yes, and we'll change our money back."

They said, "Where is your receipt?"

And we said, "We don't have a receipt."

"Oh, that's it then, you can't change your money back."

And we said, "Well what can we do with it?"

"You can't take it out the country, you can't change it back. You can give it to us or we have a store in there and you can go and spend it."

So we thought, "Why not, hey?"

So we went and bought this awful food and cheap champagne and it's certainly not given, I mean I got it anyway because we had to go and spend it in the store. But I wasn't going to give it to them. And then they let us cross the border. It was interesting. The end of my story is I went on to Australia, but my son went back 30 years later and they did exactly the same thing to him.

4. Jack Lillico – Trains

I was heading out of Vancouver and the steam locomotives were still on in those days. This was my first trip going over to Calgary. I think it must have been early sixties or late fifties. I got to Field, B. C. and in those days they took an observation car on the back end of the train. Half was open and half was enclosed. So I went out there in my suit and tie and white shirt and I thought, "I'll ride through the spiral tunnels."

Well, I got two minutes into the tunnel and I was black. I had to go and change my clothes. I looked like a chimney cleaner.

One time I was going out of Vancouver and I was listening to a football game in my roomette, and some guy stuck his head in the door and said, "What's the score?"

And so I told him. And I said, "Come in and have a drink and watch the rest of the game."

So he turned out to be a superintendent of the CPR on holidays. So he said, "When we get to Field, would you like to ride the head end through the tunnels?"

I thought the guy was telling me a story. But when we got to Field it was snowing very badly, and we headed up to the front end and the guy opened the cab. This time it was a diesel, and we got in, and I rode through the spiral tunnels on the head end.

So about two years later I was in Calgary and I walked up to the head end and the same guy was engineer. He says, "I can't take you from here because they're watching, but come up in Banff."

So I rode back through the tunnels again with the same engineer in about a two-year period.

5. *Joanne Harris – Working for the Airlines.*

I worked for TCA, Trans-Canada Airlines, between '51 and '61. When I was employed by them I looked forward to my passes. I always shared living accommodation with girls that came from Britain. It seemed to be the jumping off place, Montreal.

They would ask me if I would use some of my passes and visit their parents, and I said, "Well, it's not exactly having a visit by their own daughter or son, to have me go over," but this is what I did quite frequently.

And then I had a Scottish boyfriend for about three years, and he asked me to visit his parents, and I thought, "I'll only stay from Saturday to Sunday and go right back," because I thought, "What am I gonna talk to them about?"

One of the girls that I lived with was Irish, and she had a sister that was married to the Earl of Strathmore, whoever he was, and they lived in Glamis Castle. She told me "If you're going to Scotland, why don't you visit my sister?"

Well, when I was visiting my boyfriend's parents, I was telling them about this. They were quite impressed, but they didn't have a vehicle, so I couldn't visit Glamis Castle. However, I did phone the sister that was married to this Earl of Strathmore and the butler answered the phone and he summoned the lady of the castle to talk to me, so this was an experience.

I remember going to London one January, to the January sales. I was using a pass that was going to expire the end of January, so I had to use it. So I got to London, and I slept in; I didn't take into consideration the time change, and the shops in London were only open for another 45 minutes when I got up. Well, you should have seen me shop! I bought three skirts, a sweater, and a toque in 45 minutes. That was my weekend of shopping in London.

This old couple that I visited, my boyfriend's parents, they were quite upset that I would come that distance and just stay for the weekend, so they talked me into staying until Tuesday. That was a mistake because the airline frowned on you abusing your privileges. Like missing work just because you decided to stay longer.

One job I had in TCA was in Personnel, and I had to type job descriptions. 8:30 to 4:30 every day on a manual typewriter. Then I'd have to proofread them with the man who produced them. Well, I never had the feeling of being finished, because I would take the drafts off the top of a pile and he'd be putting more on the bottom of the pile. After two years of that my back gave out because it wasn't an electric typewriter, and I had to really work at it. So I ended up in the hospital for about a week in a body cast. I don't know why the orthopedic surgeon put me in a body cast, but I guess I needed the support, because I did some damage to my back, typing for so long. When I came back to work, I was transferred to another department. If they hadn't transferred me, I would have asked for it.

In 1960 a girl that I worked with in Personnel asked for a leave of absence for one year. She wanted to cement relations with an old boyfriend in El Paso Texas, would you believe? So she asked me whether I would like to accompany her.

I didn't think about it for too long. I said, "why not?" I needed a change of scene.

So I asked for six months leave of absence. I thought, "If she could get a year's leave of absence, I'm going to try for six months."

We drove to El Paso, Texas. Both of us had no trouble getting work because we'd been working for the airline for so long. We worked for a company called El Paso Natural Gas. It was so strange. People did more talking than work. I'd sit at my typewriter and my boss would ask me all sorts of questions about Canada, and of course, I went along with that.

My girlfriend married her boyfriend before the year was up, and I returned to Montreal.

6. Brenda Casey – The Apartment

I left Canada with a girlfriend that I'd been at high school and university with. We were both 21, and we went to Europe. Initially we went to England and got a lot of our visas for various countries. We went to France, and we were huge theatre and movie freaks, so of course we had to go to Nice, and we ended up in Cannes. That was just across the border from Monaco, so we took the bus into Monaco, and we bought some bread and wine and cheese and ate in the park because we couldn't afford anything else. We had taken with us some clothes to change into for the Casino. We wanted to see the Casino. The only place we could change was at the back of the Cambio where people exchange their money. It's a little kiosk, the Cambio. We're 21, everybody's nice to you when you're 21. So can we go in and change?

"Yeah, sure."

And we spoke French, so it was all right. So they let us in back there, so we changed and then we came out looking very nice, and everybody wanted to buy us a drink, and we said, "No, we don't drink."

We went into the Casino to see how they played, how they gambled. We didn't know anything about gambling; we just wanted to see. At the time it wasn't nearly as posh as it is now; that was in the '70s. So we watched different games, and we'd never seen baccarat. We were watching, and there was one man that was winning very well in baccarat. Extremely well, and we'd never seen anybody win that much money. He was winning enough to take us travelling for about 10 years.

So we watched him and it was great, and he was winning many thousands of dollars, about forty or fifty thousand dollars, a lot of money, and we were quite impressed. He saw us, and we were young girls and he was fortyish, so he watched us and asked if he could buy us a drink, and we said, "We don't drink."

He said, "Can I get you some juice or something?" So he got his money organized, he cashed it in. His name was Bob MacDougal, and he was working for an oil company. He lived in Texas, but he was travelling around the world for this oil company, setting up oil rigs. At the moment the one he was doing was in Iceland, and he got a carte blanche expense account, and he could travel wherever he liked, and money was never an issue for him. But obviously he was a gambler.

So we were very friendly with him. He was a very sweet man, it seemed, but then we had to go back to Cannes. So we took our leave of Bob went back on the street to catch our bus to Cannes. We sat in the bus stop a long time. It started to rain and a police car came up to us and said, "What are you doing here?"

We said, "We're waiting for our bus to go to Cannes."

He said, "There's a strike. Trains, buses, they're all on strike."

"But all our things are in Cannes. Where are we going to live?"

He said, "You have to find a hotel, here in Monaco."

75

This was all in French.

So Carol and I look at each other, and we both say, "Bob."

We go back to the Casino and find him. He's still gambling, and we told him our story, and he said, "No problem. Because I won all this money, they're putting me up in the hotel and giving me breakfast, and you can have that, because I'm staying in a town across the border in Italy."

"Great."

So he put us up in this place, and they paid for our meals, and it was lovely.

Anyhow, Bob said, "I'm staying in this town called Ventimiglia across the border. Do you want to meet me there when you get your things from Cannes?"

"Okay."

So the next day he paid for a taxi to take us to Cannes, and the taxi drove us to Ventimiglia to meet with Bob.

Bob was a very charming Texan in his forties, but obviously a very worldly person in comparison with these nice 21-year-old girls, and he took us to a couple of night spots there, took us out for a beautiful meal. In one place they thought we were paid for, so they were bargaining for us. It was quite a funny event, but nonetheless...

Anyway Bob was staying in Ventimiglia, and he got us a hotel room for ourselves. And he said, "You want to go to Switzerland?"

"Sure."

So he said there was this really pretty town called Engelberg, and he was going to meet us there. We went to Engelberg, a beautiful town, like something out of the movies. He sent us a telegram that he couldn't make it, but that he would meet us when we got to our next location.

"Okay." We didn't know where we were going. We kept in touch. We had a postal office address for his mail.

Long story short, we ended up in Israel later the next year, in 1973. We let Bob know we were there, and he said, "Well, where are you going to stay?" This was after our experience with that person in Tel Aviv. We had got an apartment; there were three guys and us staying in this one apartment. My girlfriend decided that she wanted to go and live on a kibbutz, so I was in this apartment and she was on the kibbutz, but she wanted to come and live in the city.

We wrote to him and said we didn't have a place. He said, "Well, I get a place paid for. Why don't you find an apartment? This is how much money you have. Use it to get yourselves a nice apartment."

So we did. We found a beautiful apartment. These two professors had a sabbatical in America, and they had their apartment open for a year, a gorgeous, just a gorgeous apartment that we could never have afforded, never. At the time it was about $1500 a month in the early 70s. It was gorgeous, and he paid for our apartment. For eight and a half or nine months we were there.

He came to Israel to visit us, and we took him around to different parts of Israel. We travelled as "Mr. and Mrs. and Mrs. Smith." We got a room, and he got a room.

He came a second time, and one day he said, "Why don't we go out for dinner. What kind of dinner do you want?"

We said, "Italian." We couldn't afford Italian.

So he said, "Okay," and he phones the airport and he says, "We're going to Rome."

So we get to the airport, but we missed the flight to Rome. But there was another flight to Amsterdam, so we took the flight to Amsterdam, thinking we could get a connecting flight to Rome. That was the kind of life he led. We stayed in the Presidential Suite in the Hilton in Amsterdam, and then we went to Rotterdam, another Presidential Suite, couldn't get a flight to Rome so we went to Nice. We stayed in the hotel Negresco in Nice, which was the most expensive hotel on the main road in Nice at the time.

Again, he always got us our own suite, not just a room, a suite, and then he got his own room. And we went to the Casino in Nice with him and he won more money, and then he went the next night and he lost a huge amount. But we ate extraordinary meals and then we tried to get to Macao, but I had to get back to work.

So we got back to work. I had told them I was going to Italy, and I came back with chocolate from Amsterdam and wine from Nice and all kinds of things for them from these different places or they wouldn't have believed we went to those places.

And then another trip Bob made he went to meet our parents in Winnipeg. He went purposefully to meet our parents in Winnipeg to tell them what nice girls we were. He was lovely. But he kept in touch with us on occasion because after this we went to Turkey and then Ethiopia and travelled through eastern and central Africa. He was supposed to meet us in Johannesburg, but he couldn't make it.

Then I lost track of him. Caroline said she heard from him once more and met him in Saudi Arabia. But never after that.

7. Brenda Casey – Living in Israel

I decide to go to Israel because I felt a little anti-Semitic. It is an interesting thing to describe it that way, even when I'd been raised traditionally Jewish fashion, but I had not liked how Jewish people were differentiating themselves so strongly. This country was something I was brought up with, and I wasn't sure why it was so important for Jews to have this home state.

So I thought, "Okay, I'll go to Israel, and I'll hopefully find that out."

I really hated it the first three months. I really hated it. First, they spoke modern Hebrew, and I spoke a more traditional Hebrew so I would be speaking I guess as people would in certain enclaves. Like Shakespearean. So I had to go to Le Plan. This was set up in Israel as a place for any new immigrants who would have to go to school for a morning or an afternoon or an evening depending on when they were working, to learn that kind of dialog Hebrew.

So I did that, and I got a job very quickly. It's not hard for me to get work. But I first went to meet relatives of my brother-in-law, and his in-laws lived in Tel Aviv.

When I have people staying with me, wherever I was, they just came and they crashed. In my day hippies were very common and people were hitch hiking across Canada, and I would go out from my university and pick up kids on the street and bring them home to sleep because I was a Women's Dean at university.

So I stayed with these people – I was travelling with another girl - thinking that was how we were being invited, staying there. But at the end of our week's stay there she gave us a bill. And you know, we were kids: we didn't have a whole lot of money, but we paid her, but we were really offended, and that kind of reinforced my thinking, "What the heck is this?" Jewish people are supposed to be welcoming other Jewish people from all over the world, and they're charging for it. I was quite offended.

So that added to my dislike of the country. Then I went to Jerusalem, and I got a couple of good jobs in Jerusalem. My first job was for a man who was from New York, who was the first person to do research on asbestosis. He made me his research assistant, which was wonderful, and then I became his personal secretary, which was outstanding. Then I worked at the Ministry of Labour, because he was contracted by them to work there, and at the Ministry of Labour I got to meet all kinds of people from all different countries who were working there, I suppose immigrating to Israel.

And I began to have a little bit of joy in working there. And feeling somewhat more proud of being Jewish, because this original thinking was being cultivated throughout the country. I became very close with the man who was the social worker in the Immigration Department, and he would travel all around the country setting up programs for itinerant youth.

Israel was a country of immigrants, and at this particular time in the early '70s there were a lot of Russian people being expelled from Russia. A great number from Georgia and then all the other parts of Russia, and then a huge number from Arabic countries: Syria, Iraq, Tunisia, Libya, Algeria, Morocco.

All these countries were expelling their Jews, and finally they had a place to send them.

And with that there were a lot of young people on the streets who had not been educated in Judaism very well in their countries of origin except at home. They didn't know what to do with them in Israel. So Ben set up programs for kids who didn't want to attend regular schooling. He set up vocational programs and training sites for carpentry, plumbing, electrician and car maintenance, and brought in senior citizens who were unemployed, retired or whatever to teach these kids, and because of the age gap there was actually quite a wonderful connection made between the kids and these seniors. He did this throughout the country, and I got to travel with him, to learn about how these were set up and to meet the people, and it was quite a wonderful experience.

So after about three months I began to absolutely love being in Israel and being a Jew. Because I really didn't have to explain to anybody what this holiday meant or why this was happening on Sabbath, or why this particular kind of food was so delicious. It was just a given. This is Hanukah, and this is what you do and these are the songs you sing, and it was quite fabulous feeling like you really fit in. I got a sense of what it was like to be a Christian who knows that it's Christmas. Everybody knows that it's Christmas. If you talk about Hanukah, everybody says, "What the hell are you talking about?"

There, when you say, "Happy Hanukah, chkg same'ach," everybody gets it. And you know the taxis, Hanukah is eight days, and you have this candelabra, and you light the candelabra differently for each day. So candelabra were on the top of all the taxis, and you knew which day it was because the three lamps were on, so it's the third day of Hanukah.

Or kids were walking with crowns on, with the Hanukah lights on them. You know, it was such a nice feeling to know everybody got it. You had to go out of your way to find out about Christmas. You had to go to Bethlehem to find out about Christmas, or to Nazareth.

It was a very wholesome experience in the end.

Unfortunately, I was there when the '73 war broke out. My mother, God bless her, came to visit me. I was working with the Israeli News Desk also. So I had a second job. I went and worked at the News Desk. I made three friends there that are still friends today, three of my closest friends. One was Israeli born, One was a British woman who came from Cambridge to do a PhD in Israel, and the third was a South African man who was one of the first people to come to Israel.

So, Ruth, the woman from Cambridge, was working in the Immigration Department below me. I was in the Labour department and we met that way. And we both wanted second jobs, we were both good in English and we were looking for a place we could use our English. The News Desk was looking for people to be copywriters, and that's what we did. We loved working there.

In working there I learned a lot about the policies of the country, and met a huge variety of people, It was set up in an environment that was quite wonderful when I think back on it. These were buildings I would say, maybe three or four hundred years old, I think from the Ottoman Empire. They had the Hebrew News Desk, the Arab News Desk and the English News Desk, all under the same roof. And we were right at the edge of the old city, so you could hear the muezzins for the calls to prayer. At that time they weren't electric. They are now, but at that time it was actually somebody going up to the rooftop and singing. You could hear the synagogues because there were synagogues all throughout the area. You could hear people from all different levels of orthodoxy since there were no Reformed at the time.

Everybody knew nothing against the Jewish, so it was a really cool place to work. It was beautifully set up and very ornate and oriental.

(Brenda's story of the Yom Kippur War is in Book 2)

8. Brenda Casey – Travels in Africa

I travelled in two different parts, two different episodes in Africa. One was in North and part of West Africa, but not as far south as Nigeria. The other is in East Africa from Ethiopia through Kenya to Tanzania, Zanzibar, Botswana, Malawi, Swaziland, Lesotho and South Africa.

They were very, very different experiences, because the East is more black Africa, and where I was in the North is more Arabic in many of its manners. So it was a different experience in both places.

In Ethiopia when you were speaking about your son being one of six children you were Caucasian. In Ethiopia there were not very many Caucasian people there, because the famine was rampant, and people were dying everywhere. People were eating buds off the trees. It was very dramatically tragic. Hailie Selassie was in charge at the time, and he had an extraordinary compound around his palace in Addis Ababa, where the gates were gilded and he had exotic animals in his compound, and he had pictures of him feeding his dogs steak on the front page of the newspaper, and then there were people camped all along the roads, dying.

Everywhere that you went within Ethiopia. The train station, there were people sleeping out along the train tracks so they could get any food that was thrown out. It was very dramatic.

So we were travelling in Ethiopia, my girlfriend and I, and we woke up on a train with a man stroking us. Stroking our arms, because we were white, and he had never seen anyone who was white, and he wanted to see if anything came off on his hand. Scared the patooties out of us. I slept on my friend's lap, and she slept on my lap, and we took turns, and the person was touching one arm on each of us, just trying to see if the colour would come off. He was lovely. We couldn't speak Amharic,

When you said you couldn't speak the language, it happened often in many places I went to, you just communicate somehow; I'm not sure how it happens. The heart of it. People communicate with you.

So we talked with this man and the people in the area, because they didn't know anybody who was white, and I think we got across that we were from Canada, and we showed them our badges. We were very proud to be Canadian. Everybody knew Pierre Trudeau and everybody liked him, and as long as we weren't American, we were okay.

So it seemed okay. They saw the badge and the Canadian flag, and word got along the train, and every place we got off there were people that were very kind. People were very kind to us in Ethiopia. We ended up in a very remote area with a man who worked for the World Health Organization. He had a kind of a compound that he lived in. He invited us there because he spoke English, and he thought we'd like to speak English to somebody.

I remember drinking water. The water had little critters in it, and he looked at the water glass and he'd say, "They're alive. The water's fine." And you just drink it by straining it through your teeth. The bugs go back in the cup, and the water goes down your throat. That was how it worked. But that was Ethiopia at the time. Water was very hard to find. There are some very basic foods; one was called *goona* and the other called *wat*. *Wat* was a very spicy, unpalatable mixture of beans and the *goona* was like a bread, like a naan, and that's what we ate. It was a very deprived area and very remote land. When we speak about famine-driven, a lot of it was in drought.

And then we went to Kenya, and it was again drought, but there you would see animals dead along the roadways. Giraffes and elephants in the parks where they should be lush and wild and carefree and they were dying. It was a very dramatic time to be in East Africa.

I ended up working in Kenya for a while. We went to the Canadian Embassy there, and the fellow who interviewed us had a house where he shared with two other fellows, one Kenyan guy who was a safari guide and one English fellow who was an insurance salesman for ex-patriots. They would go and meet the aircraft every time an airline came in. They knew all the stewardesses, and we got beds when the stewardesses weren't in town. And when the stewardesses were in town we got to sleep under the pool table.

So we stayed there and we worked for a little bit because they were nationalizing the country, which meant that they were becoming independent from Britain, and they wanted accents that were not British to do radio commercials. So I got to work as a commercial person because I had a non-British accent.

But we were treated extremely well there, by Ismaili people particularly. Ismaili people often picked us up, and they just had a connection to the next town or to the next village, and somebody would pass us on to other people, and we had places to stay and hotels and dinner parties and we were treated extremely well.

Ismaili people have a belief that they should do something kind for someone each day, and I'm quite sure we received that.

Also in Tanzania that happened. We were passed on to some people in Tanzania. And Tanzania was also nationalizing, and we stayed on the coffee plantation there, and they were beginning to get their money out of the country, because they knew that they would eventually get nothing back for it. The family we stayed with had a young man who fancied my friend and the young man had a friend who was a Sikh man and he fancied me. He was a lovely man, and I'd never seen a Sikh man without his turban. He took his turban off, and he had this extraordinarily beautiful blue-black hair that came down to his waist, and it was just beautiful. So every time I see a Sikh person now I wonder if he took his turban off if he would have that kind of hair. It was unforgettable. Quite extraordinarily beautiful.

In Tanzania we became friends with a man who owned the Mercedes concern in Tanzania, and he was one of those people who was getting his money out, but he also had properties that were being nationalized. He wanted us to stay in his guesthouse, but the government had taken that over. He assigned us a driver, and gave the driver whatever money he gave him because wherever we went, we never paid anything, and we drove all around the country. A very generous thing, very kindly. This driver was wonderful to us.

Only about five years ago I was at a transmission place on Broadway, and this man had a lovely accent, and I said, "Do you happen to be Tanzanian?"

Yes, he was, and he was also Ismaili, and I said, "Many, many years ago I was in Daar Es Salaam and I met this man."

And he said, "I worked for him at that time." He worked for him, and he keeps in touch with him. He's in Nairobi now. Something else, it was just an extraordinary moment. The world is a very small place at times.

From Tanzania we went to Zanzibar, and Zanzibar was a very simple island at the time. My daughter has been there since, 35 years later, and it's very highly developed and full of all-inclusives and such, but at the time we were there, there was only one hotel, which was the hotel where Graham Green stayed when he was writing one of his novels.

But when we got off the plane, they were measuring men's hair, because the men's hair couldn't be below a certain level of their neck, and if it was, they had to get a haircut, or they couldn't get off the plane. And women had to have their arms covered, so they made sure that we had particular kinds of clothing. Everybody was dressed in very traditional clothing. For the women, all black, head covering, faces were open, and most of the people wore black, but the men could go with whatever they liked. A lot of the men worked as fishermen, so they had only trousers on or short pants. They were working all along the waterfront.

It was a very beautiful, a very, very beautiful island, a spice island where you could walk on lemon grass and smell the grass, and there were clove trees and cinnamon bark, and that's the spice island I think of because it was, again, very exotic. And then there was the factory that would take all the essences of these and make little vials of perfume with the oils of all the different spices. I got jasmine oil there.

My daughter, when she went, found me some jasmine oil from Zanzibar again.

9. Brenda Casey – South Africa

After Tanzania we went through Botswana, Malawi, and into South Africa. Botswana and Malawi were very, very poor, and South Africa seemed very westernized by comparison with the other countries we'd been in. We learned quite quickly that there was a very strong divide not only between black and white, but there were 4 divisions that were in the society that were noticeable. There were black, who were called Bantu at the time, and then there were coloureds, and then there were whites, and then there were honorary whites.

To be an honorary white you had to have a major trade agreement with South Africa. Japan had a trade agreement with South Africa, so Japanese people were honorary whites.

And then within the white population there was a huge divide between the English-speaking and the Afrikaans speaking, and then within that there were divisions between who you could associate with if you were English speaking.

For example we made very good friends with a Portuguese fellow and he was a very special guy, but a lot of people wouldn't associate with him because he was Portuguese, and he wasn't of British heritage. And for sure a lot of Afrikaans people did not associate with English-speaking people.

I was with my girlfriend, and we were thinking it was going to be a place where we could work, because we couldn't get jobs in a lot of the countries that were nationalizing, and then Botswana and Malawi were just too damn poor.

And we had to make a little more money to keep travelling. We found a job because of this Portuguese fellow, whom me met arbitrarily. I don't exactly recall exactly how we met him, but literally it was on the street. We were looking for something and he knew that we were lost, and he just took us on, and he was so kind. He found us a place to stay at a travellers' kind of residence. They didn't have television in South Africa at the time, and you could only see certain movies. Everything was very restrictive. Michelangelo's David was banned, because it was a nude man. Black Beauty was banned because Black was before the word Beauty. You don't have those two words together.

It was a very foreign society to be living in. Being a white person in it was extremely privileged, and being a white girl, a foreign white girl was even more privileged, because there were so many people who wanted to meet you.

Joual got us this place at the Summit Club where a lot of foreigners who were travelling through and working in South Africa stayed. South Africa had a lot of foreigners coming to work there on contract. They could make good money there.

These folks lived at the Summit Club, and you could get a one-bedroom apartment for a reasonable price, and they had little residences that were affiliated with the Summit Club and you could come there and eat. They had beautiful buffets. They had a squash club and you could play snooker there. And then they had movie nights, and since you didn't have television, this was your big night. And they would get television series as movies.

So we stayed there, and it was a good place to meet folks, and we met interesting young men because we were new meat! We both got jobs. I got a job at the University of the Witwaterstraand in the student counselling department, and my friend, I don't remember where she got work. It was not at the University, but it was somewhere where her English was useful, and being a foreigner was also useful.

The divide was very noticeable in that the people who worked at the Summit Club were all black, and the University was all white. If you wanted to go to the University if you were a non-white you had to apply, and there was a very rigid choosing structure to allow somebody who was not white to go to the University. Indian people were allowed in more readily because they were considered coloureds. Being black there was very, very rare.

87

I went to Cape Town. I travelled a lot in South Africa and I went to Cape Town on the train and some Afrikaans farmers were on the train, and for the first time I got this line given to me a lot in South Africa. One of the farmers said to me, "Ach, man, it's not as bad as they say." And that was said to me so often by Afrikaans people. It was as though they had a sense of embarrassment and yet a sense of pride that it wasn't as bad as everybody thought it was because obviously we were visiting and we were travelling.

There were a few moments in South Africa that were very, very difficult moments. One was going to a department store in Cape Town, which was a lot like any other department store, and I went and got the things that I wanted, and went to the counter to pay for them and the young woman who was for all intents and purposes Caucasian-looking said, "You can't buy that here."

I said, "Why not?"

She said, "This is the coloured...Eaton's or whatever it was...it was some kind of store that was like Eaton's.

I said, "What do you mean?"

And she said, "You have to go across the way. The Eaton's across the way is okay."

"What do you mean okay?"

"Well it's for white people."

I said, "Well, you're white."

She said, "No, I'm coloured."

I had to leave my goods and go across the street and pick them up all over again.

I went to mail a letter, and there's two different line-ups. One for non-whites and one for whites. We all end up at the same wicket, but two different line-ups.

There were benches in the park for whites and non-whites.

And then I was buying an airline ticket and there was somebody in the same travel agency, an American guy, and he was absolutely enamoured with how South Africa was apartheid.

You've really got it straight, you keep those n***s in line and blah, blah, blah. Some of the women and men working at the travel agency and myself were just staring at him, and I said, "Where do you come from?"

And he looked at me. "Texas."

And I said, "And is this how you run things in Texas."

And he said, "It's people with noses like yours that are keeping our people down."

I just left. I left...I left.

I met a lot of Jewish people in South Africa because I worked for the News Desk in Israel, and they gave me some names of people in South Africa that they knew. These people had come as a consequence of the Holocaust, and they ended up in Johannesburg mostly. They came with nothing, but you should see the wealth that they had. It was extraordinary, just extraordinary, when they tell you their stories, and they came with nothing. Not even a suitcase. Nothing.

And the wealth that they had accumulated. I'd never seen people living in that kind of splendour. It was a real eye-opener to live in South Africa.

I met my wasband in South Africa. Peter was there. He'd been in Britain, and he'd got a contract. He did refrigeration and air conditioning, and he got a contract there for two years, and they flew him down to South Africa free of charge, and we met at the Summit Club. Playing snooker.

10. Graham Mallett – Australians in Europe.

Australians, when they used to go to Europe back in the '60s and early '70s tended to stay longer than people from Canada did. Typically Australians would go to the UK, get a job there because it was English-speaking, then take time off to travel around Europe. I did that personally. I worked for a year in London.

I think there were two factors. For one thing, at that time the economic situation was better in Canada, so it was easier to earn money to travel with. The other factor was the Australia is a lot farther away, and it costs a lot more to get from there to Europe, and to make it worthwhile people tended to stay longer. So they would typically get a job. Teachers and nurses found it easy. There were always jobs. I knew one guy who was a butcher. He easily got a job as a butcher in London. Pretty much any job you could get. I think that's the main reason.

I already was working and had worked for four and a half years and saved up some money that way. It was pretty typical. It wasn't the concept of the Gap Year, when they go right out of High School.

The people from Australia were probably older and had more experience. Plus at that time as Commonwealth citizens we were all British subjects, and we could go to any other country in the British Commonwealth and live there, work there and vote as a landed immigrant, and that made it so much easier to travel, if you picked which country you wanted to go to.

So in 1965 I decided I wanted to travel. I sold my car and bought a ticket on a ship to England, but I decided to change that and get off the ship in Italy and travel overland.

When I got to Egypt, I thought, "It's pretty interesting here," so I got off the ship there and I travelled around Egypt for a little bit. Went to Cairo. Then I caught a plane to Beirut and stayed there for three weeks and travelled around the Middle East a bit. I went to Jerusalem, which was in Jordan then.

Then I was headed towards London, where I planned to take a school, so after a while in Beirut I caught a train to Istanbul and took a train up through Syria. It took three days. I had a third class ticket on wooden seats, and to get food the train would stop in villages and people would come and sell you fresh tomatoes and things like that. You could get out and get some water and cream and that kind of thing.

We got to Istanbul. I seem to remember I caught a bus across to Greece, then I hitchhiked all the way down through Greece and caught a boat over to Brindisi in Italy, and hitchhiked all the way up to Brussels, and then took a ferry to England.

90

5. Families

1. Brenda Casey – Meeting my Husband

As I said earlier, I came from a very Jewish background and in my sisters' days my parents would not let them date boys that were not Jewish, but when I was fifteen, I met someone who wasn't Jewish and I wasn't allowed to date before I was fifteen. I said, "Either I can sneak out or I can bring him home." That was the rule of thumb.

So my parents let me bring whoever it was home.

So when I was travelling I would write them about the boys I met. And then in South Africa I met my soon-to-be husband. He was a New Zealander, and he was called a Kiwi. In those days, New Zealand was not a known area and certainly Kiwi was not a known thing, so when I wrote home to my parents that I met a Kiwi in South Africa they looked it up in a dictionary and the dictionary definition was "a prickly fruit native to New Zealand, or a flightless bird native to New Zealand, or a native Aboriginal of New Zealand.

So they had this picture of someone with a bone through his nose and wearing a grass skirt who I was bringing home to meet them, who they were thinking of as their future son-in-law. They were not amused; they were not excited about it. They phoned my two sisters, and you can imagine a Jewish mother who thought her daughter was going to marry someone with a bone through his nose. You can imagine.

So we came to Canada and the joke in our family was that they were so glad he had clothes on that they didn't really care that he was Catholic.

We met the family and everybody was joking that he had a beard and reddy-brown hair, and we just need to give him contact lenses for brown eyes and he looks Jewish, and we won't worry about it. But the family met him and he was introduced and he had a very strong accent and nobody could understand him because in those days people didn't travel and meet folks the way we do now.

So his accent was foreign, and he was a "foreigner" and then he was Catholic.

So then I went to bed. We had different parts of the house that were segregated, even though Peter and I had been a couple for a while. One night my mother cornered him in the kitchen and she was asking about what it was like to grow up Catholic. He'd been to a Catholic boy's school, and he'd never met a Jewish girl before, so this was a big thing for him, and she asked what his parents did. His mother was quite devout, his father not so much.

And then she asked were there any particular rituals. He spoke about confirmation and then of course she wanted to know if he was circumcised. But she couldn't ask. So she just kept on, and Peter knew what she wanted, and he just kept leading her on.

My mother not willing to ask until probably about two in the morning. They'd been talking, I'd been asleep; I didn't know what was going on. At two in the morning she finally said, "Well, do they do anything with little boys."

And he said, "Well, you know, it was a boy's school, so there were only little boys."

And she said, "No, no, no, before that."

And he said, "Pearl, if you really want to know, you're going to have to look."

My mother said, "I think I'm going to bed now." God bless her.

2. Deanna Vowels – Early Life

My family was a mom, a dad, twins – a boy and a girl – and me. And unfortunately my mom and my dad split up when I was two. My brother stayed with my mother, our sister was adopted out and I was given to an aunt. He went to become a pilot in the Air Force. She became a high-up something in the Navy.

Now I thought this aunt was my mother because at two you don't really remember a whole heck of a lot. We always slept together because we were always in a very small little place and I don't even remember getting fed, but I guess I did. But I got locked up every day cause she went off to work. Now, when I was six we get to bed, and it's dark, but before we go to sleep she said, "Oh, I have to tell you something. I'm taking you to your real mom and dad."

Well, she was the only mother I knew. I was devastated. Six years old. I cried and cried and cried and cried. "No. You're my mother. You're my mommy. You're my mommy."

And she said "No, I have to take you tomorrow to them."

So there was my dad and his next wife and she has a sister called Lillian. And I could remember even at six years old, this name Lillian, so I thought, "Oh that must be my mother."

Well it wasn't. It was my stepmother's sister who also had a son called Billy. Well my brother's name is Barry so that was another confusing part of the equation. Anyway, I went and lived with this stepmother and my dad for a while.

The bad thing about not knowing my history is that as you grow up and you go to doctors or anything you don't have any background. You don't know who had what. The only thing I did know was a grandmother and an aunt (we were Hungarian by heritage) had breast cancer, and they both died of breast cancer. That's the only thing I know about.

When my dad's second wife and he parted for a short time, we went back to Saskatchewan where I was born in Regina, and I got to meet my grandmother and my grandfather. She couldn't read or write. I asked her how she shopped, and she said she just looked at the pictures.

My grandfather was obviously British because his last name was Saxon. And I have no idea what her name was, first or last. I've never met my birth mother. I've never met the brother and sister. I tried to find them when I was working for the Government in Borden. I even talked to the fellas that were in the SIU or whatever and asked them if they could find anything. In fact, when I went to work for the government in

Borden, I had to get the Red Cross to find my Dad because I had to fill out a form for Security. I had to get security clearance, so I had to find out my mother's name, my brother's name, my sister's name, my father's – well I knew my father's name – and I have a half-brother who lives in Saanich. I do see him once in a while, but not very often.

It's just that every time I hear somebody talking about family, and "I had siblings and I had this, that and the other thing," I just sit here and go, "I wonder what that was like. I wonder what that would have been like." I have no family ties except my own children, now, and my half-brother in Saanich.

3. Luz Lopezdee – Early Life

I am the youngest in a family of seven, and when my maternal grandmother was on her deathbed – my sister would confirm this story because I was then only one year old – on her deathbed my maternal grandmother told my mother, "Sirine, why don't you just give Luz, – that's me – to Felix and Marcosa who do not have a child." Felix is my mother's first cousin, son of my grandfather's sister.

Okay, so it ended like that and she died. Rita Concepcion died.

According to my aunt, a couple of weeks after, maybe after my father and my mother decided to make a decision, scared that my grandmother might, you know, pull their feet if they didn't obey her wish. So my aunt said your father and your mother came with you, with a bag full of clothes and said, "Luz is all yours."

And they left. So I was given to my aunt and uncle. My mother, of course, lost her youngest. So she would come to our house almost every week looking after me.

She missed me, but you know after two years she became pregnant again, and she had a daughter so I was replaced. So in that sense, the wish happened and it was maybe my fate to be adopted by my aunt and uncle because they treated me like their own, like better than their own.

I was sent to school. I finished high school and I finished the university. My other siblings, because they were seven of them including the one that was the youngest, did not. My father was just a pianist. He would play on stages and stuff like that so it was difficult to raise and send all your children to school. So most of my siblings finished high school. My eldest sister who is now in Philadelphia finished her secretarial course and that's as far as most of them finished their education, but I finished my university degree and so I was blessed to be given away and adopted and loved because I made it. Because of that, when I got older I felt that it was my obligation to help my siblings who did not finish.

4. Maggie Gooderham – My family

I was born in England in 1923, a long time ago.

My father was a brewer. He was in the First War, 1914 to 1919, the whole of the war. He was in the trenches all the time, and his poor legs were all black from being in the trenches for that long.

He was a wonderful man. I loved him dearly. I had one sister, two years older than me. My maiden name was Fitzgerald. He was an Irishman. He came from a fairly large family. They were all so nice. But he was not happy with my mother. She was not right for him. She was English, and quite different. He was a typical Irishman. Lots of fun and very social. She was quite the opposite, which was a shame. They didn't get on at all. They should have really divorced, but in those days people didn't do that, so we all had an unhappy childhood, really. She was not nice to him at all, and she was always grumbling to me about him, and he never retaliated, which he should have done. He let her get away with all these awful things she said about him. Because looking back I would have stood up for him more, but when you're that age you don't understand these things. She was so unkind to him, and I so regretted later in life that I hadn't been more on his side, as it were. I didn't understand at the time.

I didn't really live in England after we came back from Egypt. My husband had a two-year exchange in Canada. He was a Squadron Leader.

We went to North Bay. It was terrible. It was in the middle of the winter, and we had no warm clothes, and the waves used to freeze on the beach. It was terribly cold. That's how I actually met my second husband, although at the time, of course, I had no idea. They took pity on us and invited us to Christmas Dinner. So that's how we became friends. He was a doctor. We bought a car from him; I remember that.

We were in Canada on exchange, then back to England. I had my children in England after we got back from Canada. When my husband was killed, I had spent almost my whole life with the Air Force in one way or the other, and I was cast out into the world. I lost my whole lifestyle. It was very traumatic.

I didn't go back to work. I had my husband's pension from the Air Force, and I had the children to look after. I never thought I might go back to work. I could have done, I suppose, but I would have had nobody to look after the children. I had no choice.

I couldn't live with my family. I lived by myself with my children. Heaven forbid living with my mother. I wouldn't have liked that.

My father died after I came to Canada. I suppose the war wounds caught up with him. He was such a nice man. He and I got on so well. I just wish I had, knowing the situation more; I would have been nicer to him. Not that I wasn't, but I would have told my mother off. "You're not to cheek him like that!" But of course you don't know at the time. But he was such a gent, he never retaliated in any way. Which, looking back, was quite admirable. Most men would have ticked her off, but he never did.

My father was born in England of an Irish family. They were from County Cork.

The very last time I saw him we went to Covent Garden and saw Carmen, and I remember that. A lovely memory. And then I went back to Canada. He was so terribly proud that I was in the Air Force because he'd been in the war himself. When I went home on leave, he would take me out to lunch with his friends. "But you must wear your uniform," he would say. So I would have to put my uniform on.

He was so proud, and he would treat me so nicely.

But my mother wasn't. My sister didn't do much, either. I don't think she did anything during the war. I don't remember. I don't know what she did. It was a shame. She had it all. All kinds of talent. She could paint and all sorts of things, but she never did much of anything.

But we went back to Canada for two years exchange, and we became friends with a family there, and we actually bought a car from them, that's how we became friends.

After I went back to England, the husband of that couple was very unhappily married, a very unkind wife. After my husband was killed, a year or two later her wrote and said he didn't want to stay married any longer to this woman, and would I marry him.

My children desperately needed a father, so I said "Yes." And I went back to Canada and married this man, which made my life so much better.

He had one son and one daughter, and I had two children, so we had a blended family, two of his, two of mine, and then we had one together, so that was how the family came about.

When I married him and came to Canada, we lived in Toronto. He left general practice and went into addiction therapy. So he worked for the government, fortunately for me, because I had a pension, which I wouldn't have had otherwise.

He ran a clinic and was quite successful with it.

I have eight grandchildren, I think, and two greats. I have one daughter in California, and one in Saskatchewan, and one here. The one in California has breast cancer, which is unfortunate. We don't see anything of each other. She used to come up here, and we used to go down there, but of course neither of us can travel any more, so we have to wait till the pearly gates open and we see each other again. She has two boys, and my daughter in Saskatchewan never wanted any children, so she doesn't have any, and the one here has two daughters.

6. Benjamin and Eva – 50 years of marriage

Benjamin: I'm very happy and feel very lucky to talk about my marriage that I have been here in Canada and in Mexico. In my youth, I thought that when I was looking for a wife, she needed to be someone that I loved so much the whole of my life. When I saw my wife that is here close to me, I felt in my heart that she was the one I would choose to be part of my life forever. That was the reason that I didn't do what young people generally do. Most of them only choose so many girlfriends that they don't know which one is the one they choose.

I was 25 years old when I met Evita.

Eva: When I met Benjamin I tried to get to know him well in order to get married with him. I didn't want to have any problems during my marriage because I thought to choose a husband that I wanted to be faithful to all my life. Even if I didn't know him very well, I tried my best to know him in order to get along perfectly.

I was 26 years old when we met.

Benjamin: I met Evita and knew her for three years, and after this we started thinking about marriage. On the wedding day, I always keep this picture with me. I thought in my heart that we would be okay and the future I didn't think what would happen, but if I was faithful to her and became a good man, it is like I put a seed in the soil, and after that we would get good fruit from the seed. A good, strong, plant and we will get good fruit from the plant.

6. A Full Life

1. Gustavo

My name is Gustavo from Guatemala. I came to Canada in 1985. We are a family of four children. My mother died when I was six years old. I grew up without a mother. My father married four more wives and so we are 30 brothers and sisters. I worked as a logger with my father, and when I became 18 years old, I joined the military.

I fought in 4 days of war in Chiquimula. We started one day, and we lasted four days. The airplanes came and dropped bombs a small distance from us. We went out of that place on July 24.

We spent three months there, and three years later I went to the capital city again. One day I took the bus, and I met a man in the palace. I went to speak to him. I went into the palace to guard the President for six months. One night at nine o'clock I heard three shots. The Honour Guard troop threatened to kill us. They put us in trucks. 600 soldiers in six trucks. They brought us out of the Government Service. The next day we found out why we were there. We heard on the radio that they killed the President of Guatemala, and they thought we might have been guilty. After we had been fighting with the President in Chiquimula, they thought we might kill him?

When we went to eat at 9 pm, the same person that was helping him to govern, he killed him. They gave us time to go out 8 days after this. We were there for two hours. They took our luggage and threw it out in the street. After this I didn't want to give any more service to the government.

After this I went to work in the north in the orchards for one year. I came back to my house and worked in a quarry for 20 years.

I came to Canada and after I brought my 7 children to Canada. Rudi is an engineer in Canada. He learned English in Canada. When I came to Canada I came to Montreal, and worked in the fields cutting cauliflowers, broccoli, and I learned how to drive a tractor. My work was driving the truck that collected the vegetables.

Now I am learning English in this class.

I worked hard in my country, and I work hard in Canada to bring my children here. I am 85 years old, and I ask God to give me more life to continue to learn more English in Canada.

2. Evelyn Wallenborn

I was born and raised on a farm in Manitoba, outside of Winnipeg. My dad was Austrian; he came to Canada in 1900 when he was 5 years old, and he opened a portal on the ship. Life was pretty dull. We had no running water, no electricity, no telephone, no television, no car but we had enjoyable times. Lots of fun times in the winter, specially in the winter, when we could go sledding and skating. We lived on a riverbank and so we could clear the snow and play hockey. We built igloos. I thought winter was lot more fun than summer where you just go cycling or maybe off to the beach once in a while.

Our school went from grades 1 to 11 and after I finished school, I went to college and took a secretarial and bookkeeping course. And then I worked in Winnipeg for a while. And then a friend of mine wanted me to come to Vancouver. So then I got a job in Vancouver.

My brother was ill, so I went back home to Winnipeg and stayed there for another three years. And then my ex-employer called me to come back to work for them.

They said, "We are not in Vancouver any more, we are now in Seattle." So I had a job interview in Seattle with my bookkeeping and secretarial one-girl office experience.

I met my husband-to-be at a pub in Vancouver. At that time it was a ladies' side and men's side setup. He asked me and my girlfriend if we would come in and if he could come in to the ladies' side with us. This shy girl from Winnipeg didn't know the words "Let's go pubbing," and didn't talk much. But after a day on the beach and through Stanley Park we got to know each other better.

John was employed at Britannia mines as an electrician. I had my job interview at Seattle and had to wait for my green card, after which time I worked for Western Farmers in Seattle for a year and a half. We married in Seattle in a united church. Both of us being Catholics; that's another story.

We moved to Vancouver. John's employer wanted to promote him to Chief Electrician. John said he would take that job, "If you'll employ my wife and give us a house to rent." That was accepted, and we enjoyed nine and a half years there, just short of my ten year pension.

It was a friendly small community, and I did volunteer work with Girl Guides and Scouts and was promoted to District Commissioner. I took a Saint John ambulance course and helped train the Guides in First Aid. We travelled to Nanaimo and Hope to put on competitions and they won prizes.

The mine management treated us well, putting on dances in the hall. We always had a good performance on May Day and received bonuses at Christmas.

In 1974 Britannia mines closed. Some people were transferred to a mine in Utah just outside of Salt Lake City and my husband was one of them. We moved and bought a home in Tooele. I couldn't work, as my green card was outdated. So instead I packed my husband's lunch and went off to the golf course and the spa. And looked after our one half acre; that's when my weight stayed at 110 pounds.

There was an army depot in Tooele where we often met up with friends for dinners and special events. I've been to see the Mormon Tabernacle and their choir. All our fun times ended in 1982 when the mine closed and we decided to head back to Canada, although, some Canadian families took up U.S. citizenship and stayed. On our return to Canada, jobs were scarce. My husband did some consulting work, and we spent 4 years in Burnaby where lots and homes were very expensive as compared to Surrey. Now I have been 30 years in Surrey.

3. Miriam

My name is Miriam. I am the third child of my family. I was born in 1948. The people I knew at that time were honest and sincere. The word of a person was like the seal on a certificate. I was born on a farm. We were ten children, two boys and eight girls. The girls were born first, and we were a poor family and the parents needed to put the children to work. Since I was a child, I learned to work the soil, to take care of the animals, to milk the cows. We were very poor but very honest people.

You might think that I was sad, but I was very happy on the farm where I lived, going wherever I wanted, and jumping in the river to swim.

Nicaragua has many earthquakes. We have suffered a lot from them. What I remember we have a president, Samosa, who was dictator for 46 years. He was a bad president.

We had three earthquakes. We had two hurricanes, Mitch and Juana. We lived through 20 years of wars. During this time the government made the country poorer. When I was 16 years old, I went to Managua city to work as a housekeeper. I did not study because where we lived there was no school. When I was in the city, with the little bit I knew I tried to go to night school to learn more Spanish.

My husband and myself have two children. They came to Canada to work. The children worked hard to bring us to Canada. We came to Canada in 2010.

Canada is a very good country. The people are generous to have us here. I have the opportunity to learn English. I have another group where we have volunteer people who teach us how to paint.

We are very grateful to the country of Canada and we like it a lot because your country is very beautiful. I am grateful to our teachers and all my friends at school.

4. Hilda

I am Hilda, and I am 87 years old. I lived in a town called Apastepeque in El Salvadore. I saw through my life so many good things happened to me.

I became a teacher of primary school first, and after I went to Dom Bosco University to become a teacher of Science and Mathematics in Secondary School. I finished working after 31 years of teaching. After this experience I worked in a private school where they treasure the different values of the people. I worked 20 years in this school. I have good memory of the values this school gave me, and the values from my parents. This second opportunity I had as a teacher in La Floresta I feel was a special training for me in my life.

I left El Salvadore because of the political situation. We left because of the guerillas. We first came to Canada in 2010, and we have been in Canada six years. At the beginning I became a refugee. After that a Landed Immigrant, then a Permanent Resident, and now Citizenship.

I want to learn English because I live in Canada. I would like to teach Spanish to someone who wants to learn Spanish.

I have four children. Two daughters and two sons. All have gone to the University. The sons are engineers, one daughter is a medical doctor, and one is a Home Support worker.

5. White Flower

You can call me White Flower. I am from Iraq. I was born in Niniveh where I lived with my family. We moved from Niniveh to Baghdad in 1960 because my Dad had a job that moved to Baghdad. I continued high school in Fine Arts. I finished Art School in Baghdad, and after that I became a teacher. I was a teacher for 35 years.

I got married in 1975. I have two daughters. They live in Canada. When I came into Canada in 2009, April 29th. I was sponsored by the church.

I have two brothers in Canada. One lives in Vancouver. The other one lives in Victoria. He is a pastor. I came to Canada with my husband and my daughter who was not married. After one year we got sponsorship from the church for my other daughter who was in Syria. We had moved to Syria in 2007. Another daughter came to Canada with her husband and her kids in 2010. Now we live in the same building, but everyone in a separate apartment. I have three grandchildren.

We had been in Canada two years and two months when my husband had a stroke. Now he lives in the Fleetwood Care Home, separate from me because my apartment is not safe for him. The doctor told him he can never go home because it is not safe for him.

He had the stroke on 2011 on July 11. From this time he has lived in the same place. I live by myself, now, but my grandson and granddaughter and my daughters are always with me.

We are thankful because we are in Canada. I love my country, but I love Canada as my second country because of freedom and peace, and they take care of seniors very well.

ElderStory Participants

For the safety of relatives and friends still living in their former countries, some of our storytellers have requested that their names be abbreviated or omitted.

1. *Mohammed Abadullah*

Mohammed is a student at Woodward Hill Elementary.

2. *Anne*

I was born in the Netherlands in 1923. I came with my family to Winnipeg, Manitoba when I was about 3 years old. My father was a farmer. I was brought up on a farm. I married an airline pilot, and we lived in Winnipeg and raised 4 children.

3. *N. B.*

(Name Withheld) I am from Iraq. I was born in the north of Niniveh. My city is Al Qosh. I am in my family the last one. I have 5 brothers and 4 sisters. We turned from my village to live in Baghdad. I was married in 1977. I have four daughters and two sons. My daughters, three of them are married. One lives in Sweden, another lives in Chicago, and the third one lives in Calgary. My son lives also in Calgary. The second lives in Vancouver. And my last daughter is still not married and I live with my husband and my daughter together. I like Canada very much. It is such a beautiful country. I see the peace and security here. I don't see it in my country.

My country was very, very difficult to live in. (p. 8)

4. Badayeva Family: Alex, Olena, Yuliya

The Badayeva family immigrated from Ukraine in 2003. Alex is a businessman. Olena (p.20) works in Olympic Dairy, and Yuliya (p.19) is finishing a BSc program at UBC.

5. Joan Baldwin

I was born in 1919 in a rectory in a tiny village called Chinnor in the Chiltern Hills in the south of England. My grandfather was a minister of the Church of England. My father died leading his men out of the trenches in WW I, so I grew up in my grandfather's rectory.

6. Benjamin and Eva

I am from Mexico. My wife is Eva. Many, many years ago I lived in Mexico. My three children came to Canada. Only my wife and I were left in Mexico.

I said, "My three children. What happened? Please come back."

My wife answered, "It's okay, it's okay."

Our children said, "Come to Canada."

"Oh, Canada? Surprise. It is Beautiful." Mexico is okay, but Canada is better. (p.98)

7. Beth Chan

Hi. I'm Beth Chan. I'm from Taiwan. I came to Canada in 1997. I came to Canada first for 8 years with two children, one son and one daughter. After 8 years my husband came.

My father was a steel worker and my mother was a homemaker. I have one brother and three sisters. I am the oldest sister. I have a big brother.

Some people ask me why I immigrated to Canada. Is it for the children's education? But it wasn't. I just felt curious. What is the world like outside Taiwan? So we were just interested in the outside world. So I brought my children and came to Canada.

8. Alan Brown

I was born in 1932 in Willoughby, the next to youngest in a family of 10 children (two of them died very young). I was brought up in the logging business. I spent 20 years as a blaster, and I still have all my body parts! I retired to Sechelt, and now live across the hall from my brother in Langley Lodge.

9. Tom Brown

I was born in 1923 up in Willoughby, which is close to here, and I lived there until I was three years old, when we moved down to on 200th at the foot of the hill. In total we had 8 children in our family, four girls and four boys. I grew up when Dad was logging with horses, and I loved being out in the woods with the horses. I spent my life logging, building logging roads, and working on logging equipment. I was married for 69 years and raised 2 children.

10. Brenda Casey

I was born in Winnipeg. My father came over after the Russian Revolution to Canada. My mother was born in Canada. I grew up in the north end of Winnipeg, which at the time was a very unique location in Canada in terms of ethnicity and variety and the style of life that people were making. It was the first middle class area that was formally designated as such.

I grew up with other children of immigrant families. Often both parents were immigrants although there were certainly enough people in the neighbourhood who were Canadian born and bred. It was an interesting mixture: different ethnicities and backgrounds.
(p. 17,63,65,74,78,82,86,91)

11. Niran Cassair

My name is Niran Cassair. I was born in Baghdad, Iraq. My family is two sisters and three brothers. In Iraq I worked in the Oil Ministry for 27 years. I married in 1985. I have two sons. I left Baghdad in 2008 because of the danger and went to

Sweden. I lived in Sweden 5 years. I left Sweden and came to Canada in 2012. Now I have been here for 4 years. Canada is different from my country. My country is very, very dangerous. Here it is very peaceful and different for everything. I was sponsored by the church and I came here. (p.34)

12. Darryl Catton

I was born in Huntsville Ontario, and I lived there until I joined the Air Force when I was 17. I went to school there. I learned my trade in the Air Force, and I worked as a Stationary Engineer.   (p.1, 27, 28)

13. Charles

My name is Charles. I come from Taiwan. Before we immigrated to Canada I worked in Taiwan in a TV station for 25 years. Then I retired and moved to Canada. Before I came to Canada I have studied in Japan and in USA a few times. So I have learned the Japanese language and English.

I came to Canada looking for a good life. Good housing, good background, and that's why I came to Canada (p.8)

14. Olga Crawford

I was born in Regina in 1924, in my aunt's house of all things, because my mother and dad lived in a little house and it happened that I was going to be born and she was at her sister's place so that was where I was born.

My father worked for the railway and he was an office man. My mother didn't work. I was the eldest of four children.

15. Carlos Cruz

My name is Carlos Cruz. I am from Crucero. It is 25 kilometres from Managua in Nicaragua. My children came to Canada and then they sponsored us to come to Canada. I am grateful to the Canadians for welcoming us and helping us to be here. I tell the youth of Canada, when you fight a positive fight, your country will be good.

16. Ana Dadwal

Ana is a student at Woodward Hill Elementary. (p.47)

17. Praval Dadwal

Praval is a parent at Woodward Hill Elementary. (p.43)

18. Dennis

I was born in County Cork, Ireland, but I grew up in Jersey in the Channel Islands during the German Occupation. My Dad was also born in Ireland, just after the potato famine.

In '57 Dad come out here to Canada, and they brought the 3 youngest kids with them. One of them was me, unfortunately.

We came right to Langley.

19. Dewick/Sawatsky/Hollis Family: John, Bernice, Kathy, Shawntel

The Dewick and Sawatsky families have lived in Western Canada for many years. Bernice and Kathy are retired educators. John is a retired electrician. Shawntel works for the Canadian Border Services Agency.

20. Jack Donohue

Jack is a student at Woodward Hill Elementary.

21. Ken Donohue

Ken is a parent at Woodward Hill Elementary.

22. Mona E

I am the eldest of four children. I was born in Ethiopia of Egyptian parents. I was educated in a French Canadian Catholic school in Addis Ababa, and attended university in England. I emmigrated to Canada in 1979. (p.10)

23. Morgan Gadd

Morgan is a retired educator with a long career in academic and professional theatre. He believes that expressing oneself through the arts can be a life-affirming and a life-saving activity. (p.40)

24. Ghidaa

My name is Ghidaa. I am married and I have three boys. I was living in Mosul and we had to leave in 2014 because of ISIS. They took our homes, our land, and we were kicked out. We moved from Mosul in 2014, lived in Jordan for one year, and then we applied for United Nations refugee status. We came to Canada one year and two months ago and we are very grateful for life in Canada. We are very thankful because we never expected that we would be accepted here, and we are grateful to Canada. Thank you. (p.7)

25. Karan Gill

Karan is a student at Woodward Hill Elementary.

26. Maggie Gooderham

I was born in England in 1923. I joined the British Air Force during WW II and served in Egypt. My first husband was an Air Force pilot who died in a plane crash. My second husband was a Canadian doctor who brought me to this country. (p.9,67,95,96)

27. Wanda Green

Wanda is a volunteer at KinVillage (p.49)

28. Gustavo

My name is Gustavo from Guatemala. I came to Canada in 1985. We are a family of four children. My mother died when I was six years old. I grew up without a mother. My father married four more wives and so we are 30 brothers and sisters.(99)

29. Zeba Haifi

Zeba is a student at Woodward Hill Elementary.

30. Joanne Harris

I was born in January 1929 in northern Saskatchewan, near Melfort. I was the youngest of 8 children. I left there at 17 to start a career as a secretary and steno in Winnipeg and Montreal. I came to Vancouver in 1961, where I met my husband. We married in 1966 and moved to Tsawwassen, where I still live. (p.4, 51, 59,72)

31. Nathanial Headley

Nathanial is a student at Woodward Hill Elementary.

32. Hilda

I am Hilda, and I am 87 years old. I lived in a town in El Salvador. I saw through my life so many good things happened to me. I was a teacher for 51 years. We first came to Canada in 2010, and we have been in Canada six years. At the beginning I became a refugee. After that a Landed Immigrant, then a Permanent Resident, and now Citizenship. (p. 7,103)

33. Jamilla

I am Jamilla. I have one boy and one girl. I came from Iraq in 2010. I am a citizen of Canada now.

34. Marg Kennet

Marg was born in 1943 in Victoria, and brought up there and on an orchard between Blind Bay and Sorrento on Shuswap Lake in the Okanagan. She was educated at UVic and UBC, worked as a Social Worker in British Columbia and is now retired and living in Tsawwassen. (p. 6, 33, 28, 30, 56)

35. Jeff Kin

I immigrated to Canada from Taiwan in 1997 on July 21. I am very, very appreciative of the Canadian Government that can offer this kind of living environment. I think also the equality is very fair. Also for my children, there was a good education for them.

36. Jas Kooner

Ms. Kooner is a teacher at Woodward Hill Elementary. She was exceptionally supportive of the ElderStory project.

37. Susan Kuo

Susan is from Taiwan. She worked there and in BC as an accountant. She is now retired. (p.23)

38. Isabella Lal

Isabella is a student at Woodward Hill Elementary.

39. Bernadette Law

I was born in Hong Kong. My mother gave birth to four children, all girls, and I was the youngest. I came to Canada to study Art at university, and have lived in Alberta and British Columbia ever since. I am a member of the Surrey Seniors' Planning Table.

40. Jack Lillico

Jack is a magician, salesman, mechanic and denturist, among his other interests. Now retired, he lives in Tsawwassen. (p. 54,67,71)

41. The Long Family: Sandy and Roberta, Gordon, Jamie

The Longs were brought up in the 1950s in Palling, a farming community about half way across the province between Prince Rupert and the Alberta border. Their father was a homesteader, logger, and log home builder. Their mother was a school and piano teacher. Sandy (p.38) is still logging and sawmilling in Prince George, Roberta is a retired high school and ESL teacher, Jamie (p.29,36,45,61) is a carpenter living in Nanaimo and working in the Oil Patch, and Gordon (p.23) has retired from teaching in Prince George to live in Tsawwassen and...edit this book.

42. Luz Lopezdee

I am a member of the Surrey Seniors' Planning Table. I come from the Philippines. I am here to tell a story to my grandchildren so that they will have a glimpse of their roots. (p.94)

43. Dorothea Lowndes

Dorothea was born in Brazil. At 17, she married an English engineer and went to live in the various places around the world where his work took them. She raised three sons along the way, and now lives in Tsawwassen. (p.57)

44. Jennifer Lukin

Jennifer is a parent at Woodward Hill. (p.44)

45. Middy Lundy

Middy was born in 1926 and brought up in the Canadian Prairies. (p.26)

46. Judith McBride

Judith was born in South London, England in the winter of 1949. She moved to Canada in 1974, settling in B.C. in 1976. She has worked for the last 40 years in charitable & nonprofit endeavours. Judith is the administrator of the Surrey Seniors' Planning Table and the ElderStory Project. (p.68)

47. Graham Mallett

Graham is a retired teacher and university professor who comes from Australia. He married Leda 1971 and has two daughters. He now lives Tsawwassen.

He is a 4th degree black belt and chief instructor of the Tsawwassen Shotokan Karate Club. (p.18,89)

48. Maria

I am a refugee from Mosul, Iraq. Ten years ago I was sponsored to come to Canada by my church. I love Canada very, very much. I thank God every day. I pray for Canada because here, there is peace and everything is good, not like my country. I cry a lot for my country because of what happened there. (p.22)

49. Fayza Massour

My name is Fayza Massour. I was born in North Syria, in Kamishte. My big family has my parents and four boys and three girls. I married in Iraq because my husband is Iraqi. In Iraq I had three daughters and two boys. I was sponsored to come to Canada by the church two and a half years ago. (p. 19,38)

50. Awatif Matti

I am Awatif Matti from Iraq. I was born in Mosul. I came to Canada five months ago via Jordan. I stayed in Jordan for a year and a half. We came through the church. I have seven brothers and two sisters. One of my brothers is a doctor in America and three of them are in Iraq, in Kurdistan and in Erbil. (p.22)

51. Nagham Matti

My name is Nagham Matti from Iraq. I was born in Mosul. I have seven brothers and two sisters. What we see here is different from what we saw in our country. A big difference. We have more value here as human beings. In Mosul it is very different. I was one of the people who were kicked out of her country because of ISIS. Three of my brothers have died. One of them in war, another from sickness, and the third in an accident. (p.20)

52. Kartar Singh Meet

I was born in India in 1941. I was the eldest boy in a family of 7 children. My father was in the British Indian Army.

53. Miriam

I was born in Nicaragua in 1948. My husband and I came to Canada in 2010. Canada is a very good country. The people are generous to have us here. I have the opportunity to learn English. I have another group where we have volunteer people who teach us how to paint."

We are very grateful to the country of Canada and we like it a lot because your country is very beautiful. I am grateful to our teachers and all my friends at school. (p.102)

54. Bernie Moon

My name is Bernie Moon from Korea, but actually I'm from the Philippines because I moved to the Philippines when I was forty-five. I lived there for ten years and came from there to Vancouver, because at the time my daughter was Grade 12 and preparing to go to university, so I thought the American educational system was much better than the Philippines. I chose UBC, so we moved here with two daughters and my wife, but I lost my wife about 10 years ago. Now I am remarried and living in Surrey and I am retired.

55. Carla Niemi

My name is Carla Niemi. I'm the facilities manager here at DIVERSEcity Community resources society. I'm 57 years old. I am a second generation Canadian: Finnish, 100%. My grandparents moved to Thunder Bay, Ontario in the early 1900s, so my parents were born there. (p.11)

56. Mohammed Rafiq

My name is Mohammed Rafiq. I was born in India in 1945. My date of birth is not quite correct the way it has been written in my papers. Hardly anybody from those days has an accurate date. There are no records. Being busy in his job, my Dad sent us with somebody to go to school, and whatever the teacher wanted, he put as the date of birth.

My family migrated to Pakistan in 1949. My father was an overseer in the Irrigation Department in India. He had a very respectable job. When he migrated we had to leave everything in India and walk all the way to Pakistan.

Then in 1969 I immigrated to Canada. I was hired by the Ministry of Environment of British Columbia as an ecologist. I worked with them for almost 30 years and retired to Surrey in 2000. (p.14, 15)

57. Joyce Schmalz

I was born in England in 1921, was in the British Military Police during the war, and came to Canada in 1946 as a war bride. I am an avid landscape gardener, and spend a lot of time on seniors' issues.

58. Roslyn Simon

Roslyn is a member of the Surrey Seniors' Planning Table. She was born and brought up in Trinidad, educated at Columbia University, and came to Canada in the late 1960s. (p.13, 50)

59. Elaine Vaughan

Mrs. Vaughan is a teacher at Woodward Hill Elementary. She was exceptionally supportive of the ElderStory project and organized the storytelling classes there.

60. Deanna Vowels

As you might expect from reading her stories, Deanna has considerable experience in many areas of the performing arts. Her work with many singing groups throughout the Lower Mainland goes back 14 years. She has performed with 2 trios and a duo at various Lower Mainland venues. (p.36,52,92)

61. Evelyn Wallenborn

Evelyn is a member of the Surrey Seniors' Planning Table. All her life she has had connections with other generations, and now that she is a senior, she just keeps at it. (p.32, 100)

62. White Flower

(Name withheld) I am from Iraq. I was born in Niniveh, where I lived with my family. We moved from Niniveh to Baghdad in 1960. I was a teacher for 35 years. I got married in 1975. I have two daughters. They live in Canada. When I came into Canada in 2009, April 29th, I was sponsored by the church. (p. 3,103)

63. Chong Wei

My name is Chong Wei. I was born in China in 1938. In 1948 my father went to Taiwan. My father was in the Air Force, and my mother was a homemaker. I was in Taiwan in elementary school and high school and University. I finished university in 1962.

I came to Canada in 2008 because I have one son and two daughters in Canada. Now I live in Surrey. I have two grandchildren.

64. Cal Whitehead

I was born in Canada, in Vancouver. My parents had come down from the Rocky Mountain area of Cranbrook and married in 1923. (p. 6, 26)

65. Fay Whitehead

My name is Fay. My maiden name was duBois. My father came from Northern Ireland, so we're Huguenot descendants. Dad came to Canada when he was 16. I never did ask him why. He was the oldest boy in the family and why would he leave them? I'm curious about that now, and it's too late.

66. Awatif Yalda

I am Awatif. I was born in Al Qosh, in Iraq. My father was a tailor. (p.35,44)

67. Eeman Yousef

My name is Eeman Yousef, from Baghdad, Iraq. I left Iraq to go to live in Syria in 2007. I lived in Syria for nine years. I left because of the persecutions and wars. In 2014 in November I came to Canada.
(p.22)

68. Zong Quin Zhao

I come from China, where I graduated from University. Then I married and moved here to Canada. I began to learn English when I got here. Before I studied Russian in my university. But now I forget it all.

ElderStory Committee

Gordon A. Long

Gordon is the recording technician, storytelling coach and editor of the ElderStory Project. He was born and raised in Palling, a small farming community near Burns Lake, B. C. He is a retired teacher, a playwright, director and acting teacher, and the self-published author of 9 novels. He has been a member of the Planning Table since 2011.

Judith McBride

Judith is the administrator of the Planning Table and the ElderStory Project. She was born in South London, England in the winter of 1949. She moved to Canada in 1974, settling in B.C in 1976. She has worked for the last 40 years in charitable & nonprofit endeavours.

Chanchal Sidhu

Chanchal is the Manager of Multicultural and Community Programs at DIVERSEcity Community Resources Society. She oversees a diverse portfolio of programs from settlement and integration to food security and seniors' initiatives. She has been a member and supporter of the Surrey Seniors' Planning Table since 2013.

The ElderStory Project

This project was conceived by the Planning Table, supported by DIVERSEcity, and funded by the New Horizons for Seniors program of the Government of Canada.

First we held recording sessions, for individuals and groups of storytellers in KinVillage in Tsawwassen, DIVERSEcity offices in Surrey, in Langley Lodge and in people's homes.

A second part involved our storytelling coach giving workshops in Woodward Hill and Surrey Centre elementary schools. At an evening storytelling session students, teachers and parents were then invited to tell their family stories.

Now the stories have been transcribed and will be made into a series of books.

Surrey Seniors' Planning Table

The Surrey Seniors' Planning table is an organization of seniors dedicated to connecting seniors with the community. We accomplish projects involving multicultural and multigenerational cooperation and try to enhance the lives of Seniors and promote an age-friendly community.

Other Planning Table members in the ElderStory Project:

Beverly-Jean Brunet	Bernadette Law
Luz Lopezdee	Kay Noonan
Mohammed Rafiq	Roslyn Simon
Evelyn Wallenborn	

DIVERSEcity

DIVERSEcity Community Resources Society, established in 1978, is a not-for-profit agency offering a wide range of services and programs to the culturally diverse communities of the lower mainland. DIVERSEcity prides itself on its well-founded expertise in assisting immigrants and new Canadians in their integration into their new community. Our programs continue to expand and change to reflect the unique needs of the diverse community we serve. We have a strong commitment to raising awareness of the economic and cultural contributions immigrants make to Canadian society, and to raising awareness of the value of diversity.

New Horizons for Seniors

The New Horizons for Seniors Program is a federal Grants and Contributions program that supports projects led or inspired by seniors who make a difference in the lives of others and in their communities. By supporting a variety of opportunities for seniors, the New Horizons for Seniors Program works to better the lives of all Canadians. Since its creation in 2004, the Program has helped seniors lead and participate in activities across the country.

61925331R00071

Made in the USA
Lexington, KY
24 March 2017